Ici Repose:
A Guide to St. Louis Cemetery No. 2, Square 3

Karen Joan Kohoutek

With a Foreword by Amanda Walker, Save Our Cemeteries

Skull and Book Press
Fargo, ND

The maps used as frontispieces for each chapter have been reprinted at the kind permission of Save Our Cemeteries.

Skull and Book Press, Fargo, North Dakota 58103
Karen Joan Kohoutek
211 8th St S
Fargo ND 58103

octoberzine@gmail.com

Every effort has been made to avoid mistakes, but if you find any, please contact the author at octoberzine@gmail.com, and it will be corrected as soon as possible.

ISBN: 978-0-578-19694-7

Dedication

To all the residents of St. Louis #2, past, present, and future, and the
people who love them.

Table of Contents

Foreword

I have never been granted the honor of writing an introduction until now. This flattering opportunity came to me recently when I was approached by Karen Joan Kohoutek, a fellow cemetery enthusiast and longtime member and friend of Save Our Cemeteries. The request was a pleasant surprise, but Karen choosing a *cemetery* as the subject of her book certainly was not!

Selecting St. Louis Cemetery No. 2 as the subject was an excellent choice. The cemetery is architecturally and culturally diverse, containing a mix of simple oven vaults, elaborate tombs, a fantastic collection of cast ironwork, and is the final resting place of many of New Orleans' colorful characters and historical figures.

The focus of this publication is specific to Square 3 of St. Louis Cemetery No. 2. Its purpose is to document the current state of this section of the cemetery and its tombs, to correct previously errored maps and surveys, and all the while, bring attention to some of Square 3's most interesting interments and architecture.

For the past several years, Save Our Cemeteries has stationed volunteer tables in at least two of the three Squares of St. Louis Cemetery No. 2 on All Saint's Day. My favorite place to spend my shift was at the entrance of Square 3.

In Square 3, I have had the pleasure of helping families find their tombs, hear about their family history, and watch them carry on the Catholic tradition of cleaning and caring for their tombs on All Saint's Day. Visiting a cemetery each November 1st is far less popular than it was in decades past, but in Square 3, the tradition still thrives. Of the three squares, is Square 3 that displays the most colorful array of chrysanthemums and other flowers at the closing of the cemetery each All Saint's Day.

My favorite Square 3 moment: I once saw an elderly lady place a bundle of flowers at the foot of her family tomb, close her eyes, and proceed to place both of her hands on the tomb. After a moment of silence, she began singing, immune to the sounds coming from the nearby interstate or to the sight of any of the people around her. It was a lovely moment to witness and was an example of just how connected some New Orleanians are to their family tombs, and how proud I am that Save Our Cemeteries is here to help protect these historic structures.

Because of Karen's hard work, *Ici Repose* will no doubt serve as a valuable research tool for families, historians, genealogists, historic preservationists, and taphophiles in general. She is helping to preserve our cemeteries in ways she may not even know.

Thank you, Karen, for venturing all the way down from Fargo, North Dakota (!), to brave the heat inside this wonderful, but shade-less cemetery, to photograph each and every tomb in Square 3, taking the time to conduct all of the research, but most off all, thank you for sharing it with us all.

Amanda Walker
Executive Director
Save Our Cemeteries, New Orleans, LA
July 2017

An Introduction to St. Louis #2, Square 3

This visual guide to New Orleans' historic St. Louis Cemetery #2, Square 3, will allow you to walk up and down the aisles identifying the residents of each tomb, based on publically available information largely from the Save Our Cemeteries organization and The Historic New Orleans Collection, which have been cross-referenced for discrepancies, and updated with the tombs' current conditions.

There are listings, with photographs, of 498 tombs. Of those, 113 are society and organization tombs (including religious orders), while the rest are family tombs.

St. Louis #2, located on North Claiborne Avenue, between St. Louis and Iberville Streets, was originally built in 1824. By 1847, its original single plot of land was divided by streets which separate it into three squares. New Orleans' cemeteries are often called "cities of the dead," and that description seems particularly apt for St. Louis #2, with the "city block" feel of the squares, and the fact that its tombs are in straight rows on named lanes, giving them the equivalent of street addresses. Each individual square seems like a small town, where you could almost knock on the doors, but where all the villagers have stepped out.

While it is filled with the same kind of beautiful and historic above-ground tombs as the city's other famous cemeteries, St. Louis #2 doesn't generally get the publicity, or the love, that nearby St. Louis #1 (built 35 years earlier, and home of the famous Marie Laveau tomb) or Lafayette (given publicity from the Anne Rice novels) do. Its location, bordering the site of the former Iberville housing projects and the Tulane/Gravier neighborhood, near the Tulane University Hospital, has been hard-hit by urban renewal campaigns. One is often advised to avoid the area, which is described as dangerous and crime-ridden. As time has passed, and families have been uprooted, too many of the tombs have become apparent "orphans," falling into disrepair without identifiable family to help keep them restored.

Nonetheless, the tombs of many important figures from New Orleans history can be found in St. Louis #2. This is particularly true in Square 3, the residents of which are predominantly what we would now call African-American; while some were slaves or the descendants of slaves, many would in their lifetimes been considered Free People of Color. The Square contains the tombs of people like Henriette Delille, writer Rodolpe Desdunes (whose 1911 book *Our People and Our History: Fifty Creole Portraits* is a source of information for some of his neighbors in Square 3), restaurateur Dooky Chase, and politicians and civic leaders from both before and after the Civil War. The tombs in Square 3 provide a poignant starting point for research into the African-American community in New Orleans, and the real people who made their mark on the city we love.

When the NAACP produced a pamphlet for a "Black History Tour" of the cemetery in 1980, it said that "Square 3 of St. Louis II cemetery probably contains the largest number of monuments in one place to note the achievements and struggles of Black Americans in the nineteenth century. It deserves to be preserved as a memorial for future generations." That is still true, and possibly less recognized.

The cemetery was surveyed by Joseph Carey in February 1937 for the Archdiocese of New Orleans, and he drew an invaluable accompanying map. Also in the 1930s, tombstone inscriptions were collected as a WPA project. Some inscriptions are labeled as close as "Aisle #1 – West – Tomb," although even then, it's hard to know where exactly they were counting from. Many of the notations don't even specific which of the three squares where a particular tomb was located.

Carey's map provided a framework for a more detailed survey was carried out from 1981 – 1983, as a joint project between Save Our Cemeteries (SOC) and The Historic New Orleans Collection (THNOC). They surveyed nine historic cemeteries, including St. Louis #1 and #2. That information, including beautiful photographs showing the condition of all the tombs at that time, is available on microfilm at THNOC's Williams Research Center. From their work, it's clear how has been lost to view in the last thirty years.

In 2009, Dalton Woolverton led a whole team in creating an invaluable index to the maps for all three squares of St. Louis II that are in use by Save Our Cemeteries. All the references to the SOC map and the SOC spreadsheet directly reflect back on their enormous task.

Of the 498 individual plots in this book, 120 tombs are missing. While it's hard to know for sure, it appears that most of these tombs were removed, due to collapse or otherwise deteriorated conditions, between 1937 and 1981. The THNOC survey didn't number the empty plots, so we can infer that any unnumbered plots with missing tombs were already gone at that time. The missing and unnumbered tombs with "no names" were probably gone by the time of Carey's survey.

I have only been able to identify five tombs that I'm confident have been removed since the THNOC survey, and at least one tomb – the Lopez family tomb in Row J – has been put up in what was an empty plot in the 1980s. While the rate of loss seemed to have slowed, that still means that 25% of the tombs have disappeared since 1937.

The neighborhood around St. Louis #2 is often described as crime-ridden and potentially dangerous, although I've never been bothered by anyone in any way in my numerous visits, and the presence of the nearby medical center has usually meant steady foot traffic in the area. With the demolition of the housing projects and the surrounding construction sites, it's hard to know what the future holds. Any urban area has its risks, so use your own best judgment when visiting.

However, since there are only a few palm trees, mostly right next to tombs, there is almost no shade whatsoever in the cemetery. That means that heat and sun are real dangers. Bring at least one bottle of water, probably two, and make sure to wear sunscreen.

A side note about crime: while St. Louis #2 was an imminently respectable Catholic cemetery, housing many large tombs for influential families, many of them Free People of Color, the street that runs alongside it, North Robertson, was the border of Storyville, the famous site of legalized prostitution in the early 20th century. A reproduction *Blue Book* directory, published by Applewood After Dark, lists 11 brothels between 212 and 236 Robertson, which would have been across the street from Square Three, possibly with windows looking straight at it. With the exception of one woman whose race isn't identified, all the prostitutes with addresses on this black are listed as "Colored."

How to Use the Guide: An Orientation to St. Louis #2, Square #3

Location: North Claiborne Avenue, between St. Louis and Iberville Streets, with entrance gates at Bienville and Conti Street

The cemetery is owned and administered by the Archdiocese of New Orleans. Their phone number is 504-482-5065, with an alternate number of 504-488-8681. Their web site is: nolacatholiccemetries.org.

Hours:
Monday – Saturday: 10:00 am – 3:00 pm
Sunday and Holidays: 9:00 am – 12:00 pm

Where you are on the map, and in the cemetery

The entrance to Square 3 is on Bienville. The gate opens directly onto the wide St Louis Aisle/Center Aisle. Facing the gates, the left-hand half of the cemetery is toward Robertson Avenue, and the right-hand half is toward Claiborne and the freeway.

Not counting the wall tombs, the whole cemetery contains 13 long rows of tombs (A - M, with individual "street addresses"); we are always numbering them from the point of view that we are walking away from Bienville and toward Iberville, with Robertson to our left and the freeway to our right.

Several Aisles have facing rows of tombs on each side, which gives us a "Left" and a "Right" row, on either side of the Aisle. Again, this will always be described with Robertson to our left, the freeway to the right, and the Bienville entrance behind us.

With this orientation, Rows A - M are "read" from left to right, with Row A closest to Robertson, and Row M closest to the freeway.

There are four smaller rows, parallel to Bienville on the (directional) side and parallel to Conti on the (directional) side, filling in the corners. These we are always numbering from the point of view that we are walking away from the freeway and toward Robertson, with the Bienville entrance on our left and Iberville on our right.

Square Three is entirely enclosed, with wall vaults on all sides, and a few larger society tombs in the corners of the outside walls.

The guide to each row is prefaced with a map of the cemetery, with the relevant section highlighted, so nobody should get lost.

Tombs of well-known historical figures, including the tombs noted as significant by the NAACP in their 1980 guide, are noted. But the majority of tombs for which I've given detailed names and dates are a matter of chance: who I was able to find information about.

Notes on the Numbering Systems

SOC: Refers to the map and spreadsheet of tomb information available from Save Our Cemeteries.

THNOC: Refers to The Historic New Orleans Collection Tablet Survey.

Row: The rows are labeled according to the letter designations on the SOC map, and can be "read" from left to right within the cemetery. So Row A is the furthest row of tombs on our left-hand side, and Row M is the furthest on our right-hand side.

Aisle: The names of the aisles are taken from the SOC map. Each aisle is named after a saint, which I assume was given to it by the Archdiocese. In addition, each aisle has a geographic address. The outside aisles share the names of the street running parallel to it; hence the aisle on the furthest left-hand side of the cemetery, parallel to Robertson, is "Robertson Alley," and the aisle running parallel to Bienville is "Bienville Alley." The wide center aisle, also known as St. Louis, is "Center Aisle."

The numbering of the Aisles on the SOC map is not consistent with the left-to-right labeling of the rows. Instead, the interior rows are numbered from right to left when going left from Center Aisle, and they're numbered left to right when going right from Center Aisle, so don't be confused by their designations like "Alley No. 2 –R."

For the most part, we will be using the name "St. Peter's Aisle" for that Aisle, and then either Row J or Row K, but it could be useful to know the other address if you're doing more in-depth research.

Tomb: I am numbering the tombs in each row according to the basic orientation, with Tomb 1 in a row closest to the Bienville side, and the number counting up as it nears Iberville. For the cross rows, we again always count from Claiborne toward Robertson.

For the most part, this numbering is consistent with the numbering within rows found on the SOC map, and with the SOC spreadsheet information.

However, where there are discrepancies in the numbering on the SOC map, I have defaulted to a physical count: if there are 20 tombs in the row, I'm counting them as 20. Blank spots where tombs used to be are included in the count, and noted as "Missing tomb."

For each tomb, the name in CAPS is the primary name shown the SOC map, although for a few, I have updated to an alternate spelling if that is what's clearly visible on the tomb itself.

THNOC Number: Each tomb also has a THNOC number, taken from the 1981-1983 Tablet Survey, available on microfilm at The Historic New Orleans Collection. This can be used to find more detailed information about the tombs, particularly if you're interested in architectural detail. The numbers in the survey started with Tomb #1 as the first tomb to the right, when you come in the front gates so that's St. Louis Aisle, Row G, Tomb 1. From there, they go up one aisle and down another, so you will notice that in some rows, the THNOC numbers get larger, and in some rows, they get smaller.

Where there are discrepancies in the different sources, those are noted at the end of each Row.

Name: The names directly after the THNOC number of each tomb are mainly from the SOC map and spreadsheet. Each has a primary name, which is the one that appears on the map. Surnames are listed first, with first names in parentheses. Alternate spellings are noted, since research sources, such as Ancestry.com, sometimes have name variants as well, and even an incorrect spelling or obvious transcription error, if previously transcribed, can be a clue for genealogy and other research. Names listed under the photos have been taken from the THNOC records, or are currently visible. If there are no names under a photo, then no inscriptions were noted at the time of the Tablet survey.

Wall Vaults

The numbering of the wall vaults, as used in the SOC map, is a world unto itself.

Wall A is on St. John's Aisle, the wall parallel to Bienville. It is divided into section AL (Wall A, Left), and section AR (Wall A, Right).

Wall B is on St. Anthony's Aisle, parallel to the freeway. The numbering starts with 1 in the corner of Bienville and Claiborne, and ends with 76 in the corner of Iberville and Claiborne.

Wall C is on St. James's Aisle, parallel to Iberville. It is divided into section CL (Wall C, Left), and section CR (Wall C, Right),

Wall D is St. Joseph's Aisle, parallel to Robertson. The numbering starts with 1 in the corner of Bienville and Robertson, and ends with 76 in the corner of Iberville and Robertson.

Because the length of this volume was getting out of hand, I did not separate out the names on the wall vaults in the same way I did the inhabitants of free-standing tombs. This is not to suggest they are in any way less important.

Cemetery French

Many of the older tombs have inscriptions in French, so here are some common words and phrases.

Agee: at the age of

A l'age: at the age of

Ans: year, as in "his fiftieth year"

Cit git (sometimes *ci git*): Here lies.

Decedee: Died

Epouse: Wife

Fondee: Founded (from society and organization tombs)

Ici Repose: Here lies. The word *repose* has an implication of "here rests."

Ici Reposent: Here lie. Plural.

Incorporee: Incorporated (from society and organization tombs)

Morte: Died

Nee: Born

Sous la protection (or *le patronage) de*: Under the patronage (or protection) of (from society and organization tombs)

Veuve (sometimes abbreviated V.ve): Widow

Longer inscriptions and poems are translated as we come across them.

ROW A
St. Joseph's Aisle (Robertson Alley)

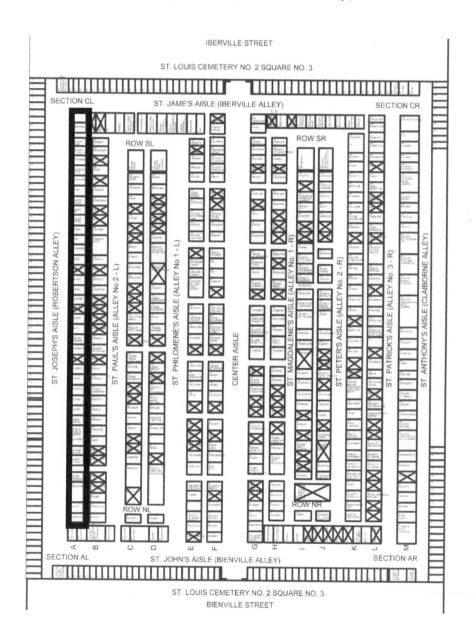

Row A: St. Joseph's Aisle (Robertson Alley)

THNOC numbers 340 – 374

This is the farthest row of tombs on the left side of the cemetery. The St. Joseph's Aisle (Robertson Alley) wall vaults are along the left side. The tombs are counted as we're walking away from Bienville and toward Iberville, with Robertson to our left and Claiborne to our right.

Tomb 1: (THNOC 374) FOURNIER (Paul); Populus

Paul Fornier
PFC US Army
World War I
January 25, 1892 – October 16, 1976

Tomb 2: (THNOC 373) PARENT

Ici repose
L. F. Parent
Mort le 27 Juin 1873
Regrette par son epouse (Regretted by his wife)

Note: At the time of the THNOC survey, there was a vase holder had read **Toulme**.

Tomb 3: (THNOC 372) TORREGANO (George V.) (alternate spelling Torreno)

George V. Torregano
Matt 3USNRF

World War I
August 8, 1890 – July 2, 1961

Note: The THNOC transcription says Torreno, but the tomb does show
Torregano.

Tomb 4: (THNOC 371) AUCOIN (H.L., Henry); CARMOUCHE (Arthur,
Fannie); Fondal; Gilbert; Humphrey (William)

H. L. Aucoin

Henry T. Aucoin
1889 – 1967

Arthur P. Carmouche
November 16, 1902 – July 3, 1949

Fannie Carmouche
January 3, 1868 – March 29, 1959

William James Humphrey
CPL US Army
Korea
January 28, 1933 – November 11, 1980

Tomb 5: (THNOC 370) SOCIETY OF ST. AUGUSTINE

Tomb 6: (THNOC 369) PERRAULT (Rita); ROCHON (Laura)

Laura Rochon
June 20, 1862 – June 30, 1938

Rita Perrault
June 8, 1877 – January 20, 1941

Stella Romain
September 9, 1865 – January 20, 1941

Tomb 7: (THNOC 368) SOCIETY OF YOUNG FRIENDS OF LOUISIANA, BMAA

E. P. Domeneck and Jos. Boyer, Builders

Samuel C. Bell, Pres
E. J. Halliday, Vice Pres
Jas. H. Carter, Rec Secty
P. C. Enamoses, Fin Secty
A. Hall, Chaplain

Tomb Committee:
M. F. Guichard
Dumas Guidry
Mack Devine
P. F. Lewis, Jr
Chas. Ory
Henry Davis
Edmond Glover
R. H. Mack Chairman
Thom Torregano, Secty To Com.

Tomb 8: (THNOC 367) GARCIA (Amelia, Melvin, Oscar, Rita); QUINTAL; Cantrelle (Olivia); Heisser (Cashmere, Lucille); Martin (Mitchell); Martine (Aline); Roland (Jean); Taylor (Lloyd)

Familles P. Garcia & J. Quintal

Oscar Garcia
Died August 16, 1961

Olivia Cantrelle
Died August 10, 1969

Alvin J. Lacabe, Sr.
Born April 29, 1922
Died May 5, 1971

Melvin Garcia
Died July 9, 1973

Lloyd M. Taylor
Died December 28, 1968

Amelia Garcia
Died June 21, 1973

Marie Garcia
August 21, 1898 – December 23, 1977

Lucille Heisser
August 20, 1922 – March 1, 1982

Aline Martin
December 4, 1909 – February 28, 1983

Rita H. Garcia

August 4, 1920 – May 29, 1986

Cashmire Joseph Heisser
August 12, 1918 – June 14, 2000

Raymond John Frilot
September 28, 1927 – December 5, 2004

Rita Garcia Heisser
June 5, 1920 – December 13, 2007

Melcolm Peter Garcia
June 21, 1916 – September 11, 1998

Hilda Mary Garcia
December 2, 1911 – March 29, 1999

Emile Garcia
Louisiana
Pvt CO D 524
Engineers
February 29, 1888 - December 8, 1955

Tomb 9: (THNOC 366) PARCHE

Tomb 10: (THNOC 365) ROLAND; LaBeaud

Ici repose
Jean Louis Roland
Died January 14, 1853, at the age of 34
La mort ne ma laisse que ton nom et le cendre.
Dors en paix cher epoux.
(Death leaves me only your name and ashes.
Sleep in peace, dear husband).

Mousseau (marble-cutter)

Tomb 11: (THNOC 364) BROCARD (Charlotte)

A notre bonne mere
(To our good mother)
Charlotte Brocard
Born October 31, 1789
Died February 2, 1838

Tomb 12: (THNOC 363) LAVAUX

Tomb 13: (THNOC 362) GAILLARD (alternate spelling Gaillaro)

Tomb 14: Missing tomb: TAYLOR

Tomb 15: (THNOC 361) TOUISSANT; Galle (Edwin family, Lelia)

Tomb 16: (THNOC 360) LEBLANC MANSION

Le Blanc et Mansion

Henry Fletcher
Born in 1791
Died October 7, 1853

With his wife
Elizabeth Laville
Native de cap. Ile de Haiti
Born on the Island of Haiti
Died November 3, 1832, at the age of 43

Mrs Joseph Baptiste
Born in 1772
Died February 23, 1850

Elizabeth Meunier
Died November 8, 1832, at the age of 70

Note: According to the NAACP pamphlet, this tomb previously belonged to the family of conductor Constantin Deberque. Creole writer Rodolphe Lucien Desdunes identified Deberque was one of the leaders of a Philharmonic Society in the 1870s.

Tomb 17: (THNOC 359) GALLE; Meunier

Edwin Galle Family

Lelia Galle
Died May 13, 1957

Tomb 18: (THNOC 358) GRANOT (alternate spelling Grenet); Trevigne (A.)

Tomb 19: Missing tomb: LANDRY

Tomb 20: (THNOC 357) BOUGERE (alternate spellings Bouger, Bougier)

Tomb 21: (THNOC 356) TRIGNY; Alexander (Jules)

Tomb 22: (THNOC 355) DePASS; Cheval

In loving memory of
Celina Dora De Pass
Died June 16, 1945

Cyril De Pass – November 26, 1956

Peter De Pass, Sr – December 24, 1965

Peter De Pass, Jr
Sgt US Air Force, Korea, Vietnam

February 20, 1932 – April 17, 1980

Tomb 23: Missing tomb: SOCIETY of St. Exaus

Tomb 24: (THNOC 354) LANNA (Arnoult); Martinez

Tomb 25: (THNOC 353) ALEXANDER (Ford); Foy (Lottie M., Manuel Sr, Manuel Jr)

Tomb 26: (THNOC 352) VIDAL; Binet

Famille Helene Vidal

Tomb 27: (THNOC 351) PLESSY (alternate spelling Plessey); Beaulieu

L. Plessy

John Beauciey

Tomb 28: (THNOC 350) DeJOUR (alternate spelling Dejoin); RAPHEL (alternate name Raphael)

Familles Raphael & Dejour

Martinez Family

34

Note: The NAACP pamphlet identifies this as the tomb of Julien Dejour, an apprentice and adopted son to slater Hermogene Raphael. According to Desdunes, Dejour came from Haiti, and became renowned for his philanthropy. "Such a man should not be forgotten. His memory should be kept alive as a touching memory." (*Our History and Our People*, p. 94)

Tomb 29: (THNOC 349) FLEURY; FOY; Barthe (Mercedes, Walter); Declolet (Odelia); Prograis (Lawrence)

Foy

Michael Foy, Jr.
Died March 26, 1973

Lottie M. Foy
1894 – 1979

Manuel Joseph Foy, Sr.
Died January 5, 1932, age 39

Tomb 30: (THNOC 348) SOCIETY BECHET; Society of St. Canda

Bechet

Tomb 31: (THNOC 347) DAVIS

Tomb 32: (THNOC 346) BASOULIERE (alternate spelling Bajouliere)

Clementine Lauou(it)e
Died August (10), 1858

(Bajouliere)
June 8, 18(?)

Tomb 33: (THNOC 345) PROGRAIS; BARTH; Escat (alternate spelling Escot)

Lawrence Prograis
Louisiana
PFC US Army
World War II

January 24 1910 – June 16 1968

In memory of
Walter P. Barthe
Born Nov 13, 1917
Died May 28, 1962

Josephine Bart
Epouse d'Antoine Escot
Decedee le 9 Juin 1833
Agee de 30 ans

Et sa fille (and her daughter)
Josephine Escot
Nee le 29 Avril 1819
Decedee le 8 Juin 1833

Odelia Declouet
Born May 16 1887
Died April 12 1932

Tomb 34: (THNOC 344) BEAUREPAIRE (alternate spelling Beaureraire)
(Hypolite J., Marie); Elger (Odile, Placide); Mix (Douglas); Populus
(Celine)

Ci Git
Felicie Beaurepaire
Decedee le 12 Mai 1850

A l'age de 33 ans

Douglas Mix
Died July 23, 1961, aged 52

Placide Elger
Died May 18, 1970

Odile R. Elger
Born August 4, 1884
Died January 16, 1975, aged 90

Tomb 35: (THNOC 343) SOCIETY OF ST. VINCENT; SOCIETY OF ST. JOSEPH

Societe de St. Victoria
Sous la protection de St. Joseph
Founded May 1, 1867

Note: Claude Paschal Maistre was a white priest in New Orleans who supported the abolitionist cause during the Civil War, among other civil rights activism. He famously officiated at the funeral of the black Union war hero Andre Cailloux. He died in January 1875. According to author Stephen Ochs, he was buried in "the tomb of the Society of Our Lady of Victory in square 3 of St. Louis Cemetery No. 2" (259), in a "gesture of racial solidarity." This is the only tomb with a similar name.

Tomb 36: **(THNOC 342)** SOCIETY OF JESUS

Les Enfants Du Jesus

Tomb 37: (THNOC 341) MANSONIE

Ici repose
Marie Monso(r)e

Tomb 38: (THNOC 340) TUCK (No name on map)

Mrie (Marie) Louise Taglasco
Wife of Francois Victor
Et leur fille.
(And their daughter)
Died May 21, 1833

Marie Louise Taglasco
Wife of Francois Victor
Died May 21, 1853, at the age of 23
And her daughter **Adele Victor**
Born June 1828, *mort le meme jour* (died the same day)

Note: THNOC has two cards for the tomb of Marie Taglasco. One says "decedees le 21 Mai 1833," and one says "decedee le 21 Mai 1853, agee de 23 ans. If Marie was Adele's mother, and she was 23 years old at her death, then she must have died in 1833.

Discrepancies
Row A: St. Joseph's Aisle:

Tomb 3 (THNOC 372): The tomb numbering on the SOC map counts Tomb 3: Torregano, as "3/4," with the next tomb as Tomb 5. That makes our count one number behind the SOC tomb count from Tomb 4 – Tomb 7.

Tomb 8: none is listed on the SOC; possibly because the space for the Society of Young friends of LA, BMAA, our Tomb 7, is so large. Whatever the reason, the number count on the SOC map skips from Tomb 7 to Tomb 9. For the rest of the row, this makes our count two numbers behind the SOC tomb count.

Tomb 19: The names "De Pass (Celina Dora, Cyril, Peter Sr., Peter Jr.)" are listed for Tomb 19 on the SOC spreadsheets (their Tomb 21), but they belong to Tomb 22. The names are visible on the tomb.

ROW B
St. Paul's Aisle (Alley No. 2 - L), Left

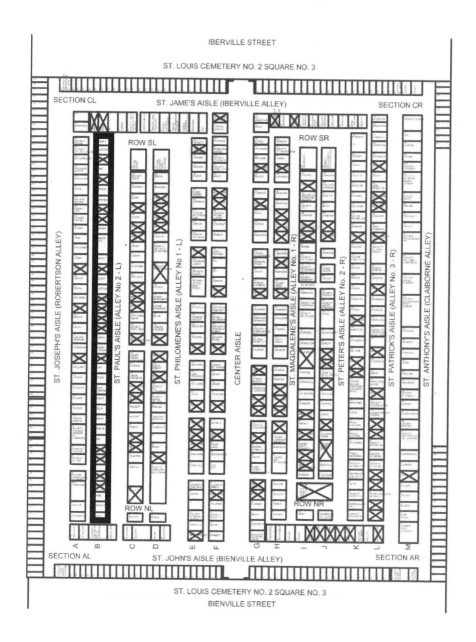

Row B: St. Paul's Aisle (Alley No. 2 - L)
Left Side

THNOC numbers 316 – 338

The tombs are counted as we're walking away from Bienville and toward Iberville, with Robertson to our left and Claiborne to our right.

Tomb 1: (THNOC 316) BERRY, C. J. Medley

C. J. Medley

In memory of
Viola Berry
Died October 1918

Grandma

Felecia Bernard
Died March 1919

Louis Berry
Died April 6, 1940

Whitney J. Broussard
Died October 20 1962

Louise Berry

Died March 13, 1941

Charles J. Medley
Born September 1, 1899; died October 23, 1966

Note: Since the names are spaced closely together on the stone, it is hard to discern whether "Grandma" refers to Viola Berry or Felecia Berry.

Tomb 2: (THNOC 317) ROUSSEVE

Family tomb of **B. Rousseve**

Ici repose
Felicite
Decede le 13 Juillet 1860
A l'age de 38 ans

Florville (marble-cutter)

Note: The NAACP pamphlet describes the Rousseve family as being long influential in the cultural life of New Orleans, involved in the Couvent school and the Plessy vs. Ferguson case. Numa Rousseve, an art teacher at Xavier University and the brother of author Charles Rousseve, is specifically stated to be buried here.

Tomb 3: (THNOC 318) BOYER

Note: An unattached tablet is propped up against the tomb, which is believed to belong to Tomb 4 (THNOC 319). The inscriptions are listed under Tomb 4.

Tomb 4: (THNOC 319) Missing tomb: FOURNETTE (alternate spelling FORNERET); Valetin (alternate spelling Malantan). This tomb has been removed since the THNOC survey.

Tablet taken to Jackson Avenue Warehouse: **Josephine Forneret** (This information was notated twice, with slightly different information).

Ici reposent
Josephine Forneret
Fille legitime de J. Forneret (Lawful daughter of)

Et de Feliciane Joulay (alternately Felicia J. Jayt) Epouse de
J.E. Valentin (alternately J.F. Malentan)
Nee le 15 Mars 1812 (alternately 1810)
Decedee le 22 Juillet 1856

J.E. Valentin (alternately J.F. Malentan)
Ne le 7 Janv 1807
Decedee le 13 Oct. 1856

Florville (stone-cutter)

(Ici) repose

Dauphin
10 Sept 1794
10 Fevrier 1842

Tomb 5: Missing tomb: MOHNEIRE (alternate spelling Monnierree)

(Photo includes missing Tombs 5 – 7).

Tomb 6: Missing tomb: COBETTE

Tomb 7: Missing tomb: ARNAUD (alternate spelling Arnould)

Tomb 8: (THNOC 320) JEAN

Albert Jean
Born December 9, 1867
Died July 28, 1925, age 57

Tomb 9: (THNOC 321) DURALDE (alternate spelling Durald)

Famille Duralde

Paul L. Potin
September 25, 1907 – September 5, 1960

August P. Casper
September 26, 1865 – December 20, 1944

Margaret Casper
October 19, 1871 – January 17, 1954

Charles D. Montegut
May 3, 1899 – April 25, 1949

Ruth Montegut
August 20, 1900 – April 4, 1950

Marceline C. Santa Marina
July 28, 1908 – November 19, 1994

Rosita P. Santa Marina
September 26, 1941 – January 1, 2010

Navarro F. Santa Marina
US Marine Corps
Korea
January 6, 1934 – February 9, 1998

Tomb 10: (THNOC 322) ARNAUD (Oscar Xavier); Diekman; Gilbert

Ici repose
Oscar Xavier Arnaud
Ne le 13 Febvier 1829
Decedee le 27 Mai 1837

Tomb 11: (THNOC 323) Society of Ladies VIDALIA, SOCIETY of B.M.A.

Ladies Vidalia Ben (Assn)

Alfred Carlin
1874 – 1953

Note: Tomb 11 is one very large tomb that takes up the space of two plots. It is counted as one tomb on the THNOC map, but looks like two plots on the SOC map, where Tomb 11 is labeled "Vidalia," and Tomb 12 is labeled "Society."

Tomb 12: (THNOC 324) YOUNG VETERANS

Finance Committee

Tomb 13: (THNOC 325) PIJEAUX (alternate spelling Rzeaux, which is obviously a transcription error).

Pijeaux – Bertrand

Tomb 14: (THNOC 326) DELAY (alternate spelling Delaxy)

Tomb 15: Missing tomb: MONETTE

Tomb 16: (THNOC 327) SOCIETY OF ST. CLOUD; Turrell

Tomb 17: (THNOC 328) HANSON

Clarence F. Hanson
Died May 22, 1940

Clara D. Leche
Died May 22, 1969

Marie D. Hanson
Died April 24, 1974

Sylvia Golis Dejan

Died July 21, 1929

Estella Golis
Died June 26, 1932

Alice Golis
Died December 30, 1941

Maria Golis
Died June 12, 1942

Gustave Toust. (Toussaint?) Fagot
Ne le 20 Aout 1817
Decede le (?)0 Novembre 18400

Marie Francoise Jourdain
Decedee le 29 Novembre 1871
Agee de 82 ans

Tomb 18: Missing tomb: POUPONNE

(Photo includes missing Tombs 18 –21).

Tomb 19: Tomb missing; TOUSSAINT

Tomb 20: Missing tomb: POPULUS

Tomb 21: Missing tomb: EMERSON

Tomb 22: (THNOC 329) LACROUIX

Tomb 23: (THNOC 330) SOCIETY of St. Angele

Tomb 24: Missing tomb: SOCIETY of St. A. and St. A.

Tomb 25: (THNOC 331) ARNAULT (alternate spelling Arnoult)

Tomb 26: (THNOC 332) FRANCIS, DYER; Society & Mutuel de L'Equite Francis

Francis Family

Mama
3-12-12
8-11-77

In memory of **Sister Theresa Francis**

The Lord is My Sheperd (sic)
I Shall Not Want
Jacob Joseph Francis, Sr.
September 18, 1910 – January 3, 1995

Hypolite Francis, Jr.
Tec 4 US Army
World War II
July 5, 1915 – March 4, 1997

Theresa S. Francis
1912 - 1977

Bennie Francis, Sr.
Tec 4 US Army
World War II
July 26, 1922 – June 25, 2007

Dolores M Dyer
1933 – 1991

Rest in Peace
Ethel J. Barbarin Francis

December 12, 1908 – August 8, 1980

Celeste J. Francis
October 13, 1913 – September 2, 1996

Joseph Henry Francis
April 1, 1944 – September 11, 2010

Tomb 27: (THNOC 333) FORTIER

Famille de Mrs. V. Pizero

Tomb 28: Missing tomb: CARLON (alternate spelling Carlong)

(Photo includes missing Tombs 28 – 29).

Tomb 29: Missing tomb: DUSUAU

Tomb 30: (THNOC 334) CARPANTIER; Garand

Ici repose
Rose Garaud
Decedee le 28 Nov 1851, agee de quatre vingt ans (80 years)

Marie Garaud
Ici repose

Antoine S. Carpantier
Decedee le 11 Avril 1830, l'age de 60 ans

Tomb 31: (THNOC 335) FRANCIS; Francoise (J. Louis Francoise) (alternate spelling Francois); Rouzan

In memory of my dear husband
Alfred Francis
Died July 7, 1939

Ici repose
J. Louis Francois
Decede le 27 Janv 1845
A l'age de 27 ans

Louis J. Rouzan
Died January 20, 1939

Helen Velina LeBlanc Rouzan
October 5, 1914 – June 14, 1996

Helen F. Doyle
May 13, 1929 – February 23, 1998

Mildred F. Ferguson
March 26, 1922 – September 15, 2003

Harold S. Rouzan
July 16, 1911 – December 28, 2003

Ethel Francis
June 28, 1919 – February 4, 1977

Florville

Tomb 32: Missing tomb: PIERRY (alternate spelling Pierre)

Tomb 33: (THNOC 336) REMY

Remy

Elisee + Rillieux
Nee le 30 Octobre 1833 decede le 22 Juin 1872

Elizabeth Wiltz
Epouse de Valmont Deslonde
Et sa mere

Marianne Frederick

Evilina Rillieux
Nee le 1 Mai 1837
Decede le 4 Dec 1853

Tomb 34: Missing tomb: CARRERE; Rodolphe

Tomb 35: (THNOC 337) PFLUEGER; Cheval

Pflueger

Tomb 36: (THNOC 338) MASSET (alternate spelling Mosset)

Masset-Christophe

Dinet Families

Emile A. Bicard
Died July 13, 1924, aged 66 yrs

Angelique Mosset
Morte le 10 Janvier 1841

Hypolite Lacorbiere
Mort le 10 Juillet 1851

Marie Lacorbiere
Epouse de L. Soublet
Mort le 11 Juin 1887 a l'age de 24 ans

Omer Dinet
Louisiane
S I US Navy

Discrepancies
Row B: St. Paul's Aisle

Tomb 3 (THNOC 318): The unattached closure table listed as propped at
Tomb 3 in 1983 apparently belonged to Tomb 4 (THNOC 319). The
information on that tablet was transcribed twice, clearly for the same

person, but slightly differently. Both sets of information have been listed under Tomb 4.

Tomb 4 (THNOC 319): was numbered in 1980, but it's crossed off on the SOC map.

The tomb numbering begins to diverge between the SOC map and spreadsheet after Tomb 11. The map shows three society tombs in a row: St. Vidalia at Tomb 11, Society of BMA at Tomb 12, and the Young Veterans at Tomb 13. The spreadsheet has "Rzeaux" at Tomb 13; probably an error for Pijeaux, which is Tomb 14 on the map. The tomb number on the spreadsheet continues to be one behind the number on the map until Tomb 27, a large tomb which the Tablet Survey lists as "the Francis Family." The map shows it as "Francis, Dyer," and the spreadsheet has both "Francis" and "Society de Mutuel et L'Equite Francis." The map suggests that Francis and Dyer are two separate names; the spreadsheet shows "Francis Dyer," as if it's one person.

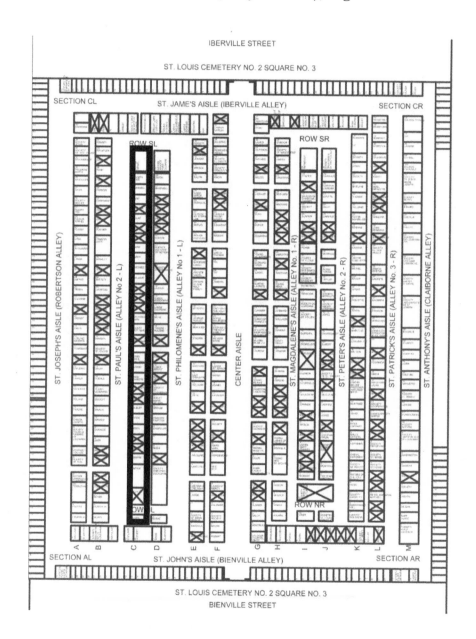

Row C: St. Paul's Aisle (Alley No. 2 - L)
Right Side

THNOC numbers 296 – 315

The tombs are counted as we're walking away from Bienville and toward Iberville, with Robertson to our left and Claiborne to our right.

Tomb 1: (THNOC 315) **SOCIETY of Perseverance**

Tomb 2: Missing tomb: KAERY

Tomb 3: (THNOC 314) ARMOUR; Prieto

Leo J Armour
PFC US Army
January 16, 1922 – October 44 1973

William Laurence
Son of Thomas and Elizabeth Laurence
Of Long Island
(State of) New York
(died in) this city
(the 16.th) August 1804
(the 22.nd year) of his age

Note: the cemetery was consecrated in 1823. It's possible that William Laurence was moved later. This inscription is no longer visible.

Tomb 4: (THNOC 313) COBETTE (Alphonse D., Alton, Jr., Caliste, Caroline, Fernand E., Fernand, Jr., Rita Jean, Ruiz, Sr., Wilford P.) (alternate speling Caubette); Cobette-Bartau (Julia); Malava (Alex)

Cobette Family

Caliste Caubette
Ne au con-Francois
De-d' Haiti
Decede le 11 Novembre 1839
A l'age de 50 ans

Alton T. Cobette, Jr.
March 26, 1934 – September 28, 1963

Fernand E. Cobette, Jr.
July 9, 1897 – August 9, 1983

Julia Cobette Bartaux
November 17, 1901 – September 26, 1982

Alphonse D. Cobette
December 16, 1898 – November 25, 1984

Loretta Cobette Meyers
August 4, 1914 – March 13, 1996

Fernand E. Cobette
Born in 1876; died July 8, 1918

Alex. Malava
Died November 19, 1923, aged 27 years

Ruiz Cobette, Sr.
Born August 4, 1878; died April 21, 1925

Wilford P. Cobette
Born May 17, 1928; died December 29, 1937

Rita Jean Cobette
Born May 30,1876; died February 5, 1954

Caroline Cobette
1879 – 1964

Tomb 5: Missing tomb: SOCIETY of Pabon Couseil

(Photo includes missing Tombs 5 – 6).

Tomb 6: Missing tomb: VIVIANT

Tomb 7: (THNOC 312) CHEVAL; Desdunes (alternate spelling Desoumes); Frere

Cheval and Desdunes and Frere families

Note: The NAACP pamphlet verifies this as the resting place of noted Creole author Rodolphe Lucien Desdures, 1849 – 1928. His book, *Our People and Our History: Fifty Creole Portraits*, is an important source about his times, and specifically about some of his neighbors in Square 3.

Also, this tomb has been said to house the remains of Marie Laveau's daughter, frequently known as Marie II, but I have been unable to locate any confirmation of this outside the book *Women and New Orleans*, by Mary Gehman. She states that a historian recently placed her "in a different tomb a few feet away under the name Mrs. Charles Laveau," but that tomb isn't identified (p. 30).

Tomb 8: (THNOC 311) WOODS (Anna C.)

Charles Lesassier
Mort le 16 (or 18) Dec 1907

Stanley A. Saulny (?), Sr.
September 10, 1920 – January 7, 1948

Anna C. Woods
September 1, 1918 – October 21, 1984

Tomb 9: (THNOC 310) DOUBLET; Brule

Tomb 10: Tomb missing: SOCIETY of Morale Character; Baham (Peter F.); Bourgeau (Lise C.); Boutte (Annabell); Chase (Charles, Doris M., Edgar L. Dooky, Sr., Emily, Joy M.); Chase-Tennette; Davis (David H. Sr., Vera T.); Ranson (E.A.); Russel (Irene); Tennette (Arthur, Emile, Ermine, Joseph A. Sr.)

(Photo includes missing Tombs 10 – 11).

Tomb 11: Tomb missing: LARONCHERE (alternate spelling Aronchere)

Tomb 12: (THNOC 309) CHASE, TENNETTE; Coussy

E.A . Ranson
1852 – 1916
(possibly the A. Emson noted by the Survey)

Emile Tennette
1882 – 1936

Arthur Tennette
1904 – 1937

Aurelia Chase
1889 – 1947

Joy M. Chase
1948 – 1948

Irene Russell
1872 – 1951

Peter F. Baham
1889 0 1954

Annabell Boutte
1915 - 1956

Edgar L. Dooky Chase Sr.
January 23, 1901 - February 21, 1958
Buried February 24, 1958

David H. Davis, Sr.
1909 - July 13, 1965

Charles Chase
1898 – 1966

Ermine Tennette
1883 – 1967

Joseph A. Tennette, Sr.
1895 – 1972

Lise Bourgeau
June 8, 1903 - September 28, 1972

Vera T. Davis
1908 – 1985

Doris M. Chase

1927 – 1990

Emily Chase
1906 – 1992

Karl G. Davis
1952 - 2010

Note: Edgar L. Dooky Chase, Sr. and his wife Emily founded the famous Dooky Chase's Restaurant in 1941.

Tomb 13: (THNOC 308) LAVIGNE (Victor and Family)

Famille Victor Lavigne
A notre Mere

V ve Victor Lavigne
Decedee le ? Septembre 1902

Note: There was a prominent Victor Lavigne, an African-American Union Army officer (serving in the 73rd USCT) who "became a noted spiritualist," according to Stephen J. Ochs (*A Black Patriot and a White Priest* 65). I have been unable to find any information about the burial or exact date of death of this Victor Lavigne.

Tomb 14: (THNOC 307) Society of LADIES' VENUS STAR, BMAA

Ladies Venus Star B.M.A.A.

Alice Holmes, Pres
Louis A. Powell, Vice Pres
Louis J. Foster, Rec Sec
H. O. Monette, Fin Sec
Paul Bermann, Asst Sec
Emily Holmes, Chairlady, Fin Sec
Mary Martin, No 1 Chairlady, R. Com
Antoine ( )

Tomb Com
A. Holmes Ex Officio
L. J. Foster Chman
O. J. Felix Asst
L. Metye
M. Martin
A. Johnson
H. O. Monette Sec to Com

Tomb 15: Tomb missing: SOCIETY OF DETERMINATION

Tomb 16: (THNOC 306) Ladies PROTECTIVE B.M.A.A. (alternate spelling Society of Protirem)

Ladies Protective BMAA

Tomb 17: (THNOC 305) ESPERANCE; SMITH

Tomb 18: Tomb missing: SOCIETY of Protective

(Photo contains missing Tombs 18 – 20)

Tomb 19: Tomb missing: DIAZ (alternate spelling Diez); Muller

Tomb 20: Tomb missing: VIRGILE; Fuller (Roy); L'Lopis (Ernestine)

Tomb 21: (THNOC 304) MEILLEUR; Andry; Bloom (Grace A.); Calhoun (Louise Andry); Coulon (Coralie Lemoine); Landry (Richard); Lemoine (A., Alcest, Z.)

Tomb 22: (THNOC 303) MARTINEZ

E Meilleur (first name may be Henry)
Note: That speculation came from THNOC.

(?) S Meilleur

Tomb 23: (THNOC 302) LAZIAN (alternate spelling Lezian); Cayatan

In memory of my darling husband
Roy Fuller
Died March 13, 1957

Ernestine F. L'Lopis
Died February 27, 1949

Tomb 24: (THNOC 301) ANDRY; Dauphin

Andry Famille

Coralic Lemoiine Coulon
November 6, 1885 – November 16, 1944

Grace A. Bloom
August 20, 1917 – August 16, 1945

Louise

Z. Lemoine
1858 – 1933

A. Lemoine
1890 – 1936

Louise Andry Calhoun
1913 – 1937

Richard Andy
Apr 3, 1871 – Aug 7, 1942

Alcest Lemoine
Died June 16, 1950

Tomb 25: Tomb missing: PELASIE (alternate spelling Pelagie); Kernion (Francois)

(Photo includes missing Tombs 25 – 26)

Tomb 26: Tomb missing: HARANG; Cezard (Charlotte); Marrero (Arthur J.)

Tomb 27: (THNOC 300) COUAIT

Tomb 28: Tomb missing: PAYRAUX (alternate spelling Peyroux, Peyraux)

Tomb 29: (THNOC 299) BADIE

Celestin (J)uin, Juillet 1833

Valerie Badie, 16 Fev 1845

Mellia Badie (___)

Joseph Badie, Aout 1846

Celeste Badie, Juin 1849

Gustave Badie, Avril 1849

Celestin Juin, (___) 1849

Ici repose
Francois Kernion
Du Conho M. MM.
Decedee le 20 Juillet 1838
Age de 84 ans.

Tomb 30: (THNOC 298) MARRERO; Cezar (alternate spelling Cenas)

Antoinette Mattews
February 6, 1884 – January 27, 1955

Antoine Mattews
September 4, 1881 – February 6, 1959

Ci Git
Charlotte Cezard
D'ile Cez Arene

Arthur J. Marrero
Louisiana
Pvt US Army, World War I
January 15, 1896 – September 26, 1964

Mary Marrero
December 3, 1872 – December 26, 1957

Aurelia Boissier Randolph
November 15, 1881 – November 16, 1961

Walter J. Pascal, Jr.
February 14, 1919 – January 30, 1975

Andrew Leo Madere
March 4, 1901 – August 18, 1977

America Marrero Madere
January 1, 1900 – November 22, 1986

Anita Leontine Madere
March 3, 1927 – May 17, 2003

Tablet leaning against tomb:
Consacre a la memoire (Sacred to the memory of)
Marie Ansteve
Surnomme Ado (surname Ado)
Decedee le 26 Fevrier 1832
A l'age de 60 ans.

Tomb 31: (THNOC 297) SOCIETY OF SANTI

Tomb 32: (THNOC 296) PEPPIN (alternate spelling Pepin, Pepan), (Aurelia, Walter J.); DANIEL (Viola P.); Freyd

In memory of
Walter J. Pepin
Died January 17, 1920

Aurelia Pepin
Died August 30, 1933

Viola P. Daniel
1887 – 1970

Discrepancies
Row C: St. Paul's Aisle

On the SOC map, there's an inconsistency: it shows Tomb 1, then a gap, identified as Row NL. When it starts counting the tombs again, the first is a crossed-out Tomb 12, followed by Tomb 2 (Armour). The identification of Armour is consistent in the different sources. St. John's Aisle, Row NL, Tomb 12 is listed in the spreadsheet as Kaery; which was clearly the name put on the map, then crossed out.

The presence of this extra tomb in the row puts my numbering system one ahead of the numbering system on the map and spreadsheet, which is consistent starting at Tomb 2: Armour (our Tomb 3).

The map and spreadsheet then diverge from each other between our Tombs 7 and 9.

The plot thickens at the map's Tomb 6 (our tomb 7), showing Cheval, which the speadsheet shows as Desoumes and Woods. The map's Tomb 7 shows as Woods, which the spreadsheet shows as Doublet and Brule. The map's Tomb 8 shows as Doublet, and the spreadsheet shows as No Name. After that, the map and spreadsheet match, although they are still off in my numbering, thanks to the Tomb 12 mentioned above.

Tomb 10: The SOC spreadsheet information includes information that clearly belongs to Tomb 12.

Tomb 11: The SOC map shows a missing tomb, with the name crossed off. The name clearly starts with an "A," and appears to be "Aronchere." The handwritten map this was based on does show "Laronchere," with the "L" slightly off-set.

Tomb 20: The SOC spreadsheet puts the names Roy Fuller and Ernestine L'Lopis at this tomb. The THNOC information shows those names at Tomb 23 (THNOC 302). A tombstone with those names is currently at Tomb 23, but it has been damaged and is detached from the tomb itself. So it's hard to say if the names were transcribed incorrectly on the spreadsheet, or if the stone was moved from the area of the missing Tomb 20 to the front of Tomb 23.

Tomb 21: It appears that, on the spreadsheet, this tomb got the names from the Andry Famille put there instead of on Tomb 24 (THNOC 301). The names associated with Tomb 21 in my count, the end "Peppin, Daniel" tomb, were added onto the Peyreaux tomb information (map/spreadsheet Tomb 27, my Tomb 28). The map shows this tomb at St. James's Aisle, Row SL, Tomb 15, and the spreadsheet gives that as "Freyd."

Tomb 29: The THNOC information shows Francois Kernion in this tomb, but the SOC spreadsheet puts Francois Kernion in the missing tomb 25. It's possible again that the front tablet was moved from site of tomb 25 to the front of tomb 29.

ROW D
St. Philomene's Aisle (Alley No. 1 - L), Left

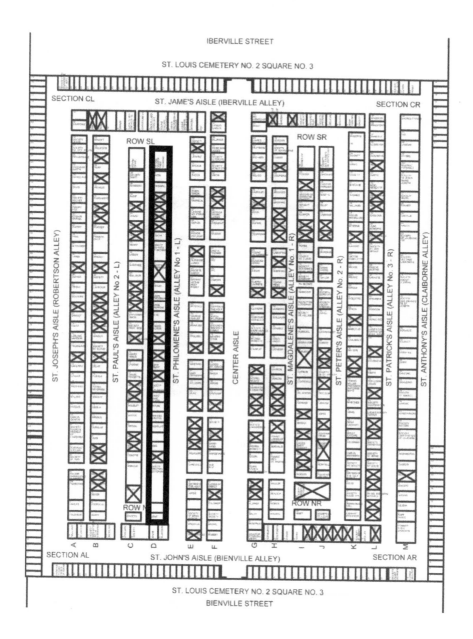

Row D: St. Philomene's Aisle (Alley No 1 - L)
Left Side

THNOC numbers 274 – 295

The tombs are counted as we're walking away from Bienville and toward Iberville, with Robertson to our left and Claiborne to our right.

Tomb 1: (THNOC 274) BURKE (Leola M.); Barthe   (Gertrude D.); Blanchard (B.F., Louis, Louis P.); Davis (Chas., Pauline F.); Duf Auchard (G.A.); Guichard; Lewis (Felix); Marceline (Henry)

Leola Marie Burke
Died January 16, 1919, aged 6 years

Tomb 2: (THNOC 275) SOCIETY OF CHRISTIAN DOCTRINE

Christian Doctrine Society

In loving memory of my dear mother
Mrs. Ophelia Francis
Born September 25, 1884
Died November 21, 1968

In loving memory of our dear mother
Mrs. Marguerite A. Smith
Born September 24, 1881
Died July 21, 1958

Tomb 3: Tomb missing: CAZEAU (alternate spelling Cazeaux); Francis (Ophelia); Keppard (Mary)

Tomb 4: (THNOC 276) MOSS (alternate spelling Mose); Nolasco (Moss)

Nolasco – Moss

W. J. Molless
Died May 8, 1906

W. J. Nolasco
Died May 12, 1908
A. L. Nolasco
Died February 26, 1912

Ellen D. Moss
Died September 11, 1915

Tomb 5: (THNOC 277) No name

Tomb 6: (THNOC 278) CAGNOLATTI (alternate spelling Cagnolat) (Anna, Ernie "Lil Cag", Leon, Ruth Johnson, Rev. Uster); Cagnolatti Maheia (Junita); Cagnolatti-Scorza (Inez); Fazande; Holmes (Robert Bernard); Keller (Claudia, Rev. B. V.); Maheia (Elihu); Scorza-Maker (Catherine); Shelby (Robert B.)

In memory of
Anna Cagnolatti
Born July 26, 1876; died June 2, 1949

Leon Cagnolatti

Born August 4, 1876; died August 5, 1958

Inez Cagnolatti Scorza
September 23, 1897 – August 12, 1982

Robert Bernard Holmes
June 4, 1926 – January 16, 1997

Rebecca Johnson Holmes
February 20, 1932 – January 11, 2013

In memory of my wife
Catherine Scorza Maker
December 10, 1923 – April 12, 1973

Ernie "Lil Cag" Cagnolatti
April 2, 1911 – April 7, 1983

Claudia C. Keller
February 26, 1909 – December 23, 1997

Juanita Cagnolatti Maheia
February 13, 1905 – December 23, 1989

Ruth Johnson Cagnolatti
August 8, 1906 – March 21, 2009

Wilma Scorza Reimoneno
August 13, 1920 – July 17, 2012

Rev. B. V. Keller
Laid to Rest
February 29, 1972

In Memory of my husband
Elihua Maheia
May 13, 1897 – April 13, 1959

In memory of our brother
Robert B. Shelby
February 13, 1898 - November 30, 1966

Rev. Lester F. Cagnolatti
Louisiana
T. Sgt. Ordnance Department
World War II
January 12, 1908 – January 15, 1962

Note: There are two men buried here with the honorific "Rev.," which I'm more used to in a Protestant context. However, various sources agree that it is a formal title for a Catholic priest.

Tomb 7: (THNOC 279) GARDERE (Emma, Ernest); CLAYTON (Robert, Romona); Le Languu (alternate spelling Languule) (Mary Louise)

Marie Louise Languule
Died August 15, 1871

Ernest Gardere
Died September 17, 1922

Emma Gardere
Died May 12, 1932

Robert Clayton
Died May 29, 1987

Romona Clayton (alternate name Ramonia Gardere Clayton)
Died August 23, 1946

Tomb 8: (THNOC 280) BROWN

Tomb 9: (THNOC 281) SOCIETY MARIE ST. ANN (alternate name Society of St. Ann, Societe Marie Ste Aane); Adler (Felicie Marie, James Edward, Jr.)

Societe Marie Ste Anne

Felicie Mary Adler
July 3, 1902 – December 19, 1980

James Edward Adler Jr.

August 8, 1904 – August 8, 1977

Fondee le 7 Sept 1857

Tomb 10: (THNOC 282) SOCIETY OF ST. CATHERINE; Societe Des Dames Naites de la Louisiane

Societe Des Dames Naites de la Louisiane

Tomb 11: Tomb missing: SOCIETY OF COR JESUS

Tomb 12: (THNOC 283) LABAT (Casimir Sr., Casimir Jr., Laura, M. Felonise); BENOIT (J. Emelia)

Ci-git
M. Felonise Labat
Epouse de Seaphin Beaulieu
Morte le 21 Avril 1840
Age de 36 ans

My Dear Husband
Anthony Grandpre
January 17, 1893 – May 23, 1950

J. Emelia Benoit
Epouse de Casimir Labat
Nee le 19 Oct 1818
Decedee le 29 Janv 1837

Laure Labat

Casimir Labat, Jr

Casimir Labat, Sr
Decedee le 13 Fev 1881 age de 70 ans

Tomb 13: Tomb missing: DUPUY; Lange (Margie Roche, Wilton H. Sr.)

(Photo includes missing Tombs 13 – 14).

Tomb 14: Tomb missing: VERRET; Chancellor (Sheila); Bordenave (Christopher Jr, Jeanne)

Tomb 15: (THNOC 284) THEZAN; ROUSSE; Hall (Leontine R.); Henry (Hilda H.); St. Latour (Claire F.); Remy (Rose E.)

Familles Rousseau et Thezan

In memory of **Arnold J. Augustine**
Born October 26, 1907
Died February 18, 1978

Ici + Git
Leonine Thezan

Ci Git
Rose T(__) Thezan
Nee a (__) Cuba
Le 19 Avril 1801
Decedee le (__) Aout 1927

Alex Nelder (stone cutter)

Tomb 16: (THNOC 285) MILNE

Raymond Family

Lang

Rousseau

Marion Labeaux
1923 A. T. Daniel 1976
Funeral Home

Tomb 17: (THNOC 286) LANGE; DAUPHINE; Cerre (Dora); Dubuclet (Chantelle); Dynum (Olvia N.); Fouche (Johnville, Marie Cerre); Marioun (P. Ch.); Perkins (Jay, Sr.); Saloy (Cora Cerre)

G. Roche, Jr.

Ici repose
Jules Dauphin
Decedee le 28 Juillet 1810

Wilton H. Lange, Sr.
Nov. 3, 1921 – Nov. 19, 1996

Margie Roche Lange
April 6 1921 – Jan. 29 2006

Note: The cemetery was consecrated in 1823. It's possible that Jules Dauphin was moved later into a newer family tomb.

Tomb 18: (THNOC 287) ALDER; BORDENAVE (alternate spelling Bordenav); Bakewell; Ducloslance (M. Louise)

Chris J. Bordenave, Sr.
October 25, 1892 – January 6, 1958

Sheila B. Chancellor
1963 – 1987

Jeanne Bordenave
1922 – 1989

Jerome Bordenave
1957 – 1990

Christopher Bordenave, Jr.
1914 – 1993

Benjamin A. Bordenave
1925 – 1998

Gary A. Bordenave
1953 – 2002

Alvin J. Bordenave, Jr.
1919 – 2004

Beulah L. Bordenave
1923 – 2010

Tomb 19: (THNOC 288) LATOUR; Davina (Wille); Johnson (Mary); Millon (Joseph, Jr.); Simon (J.J.); Thomas (Antonia)

Ici Repose
St. Claire F. Latour
Decedee le 12 Janvier 1840
A l'age de 33 ans

Rose E. Remy
February 15, 1908 – June 12, 1972

Leontine R. Hall
Born May 24, 1914; died June 14, 1985

Hilda H. Henry
October 2, 1902 – March 21, 1991

Note: It's unclear whether St. Claire is a first name associated with the surname Latour, or the surname of another person.

Tomb 20: Tomb missing: SOCIETY OF ST. PHILOMENE

Tomb 21: (THNOC 289) SOCIETY LES ARTS OF METIERS; Eustis (Henry)

Tomb 22: (THNOC 290) FOUCHE; Marieux; Dubuclet

Ici repose le depouille mortelle de
(Here lie the mortal remains of)
P. Ch. Marioux
Ne a St. Marcelle St. Dominique
Rep. d'Hayti
Le 20 Octobre 1775
Decede le 4 Octobre 1839

Jay Perkins, Sr.
1904 – 1959

Johnville Fouche
1886 – 1971

Chantelle Dubuclet
1977 – 1977

Olivia N. Bynum
1912 – 1995

Christine N. Adams
1948 - 2013

Tomb 23: Tomb missing: PATY

(Photo includes missing Tombs 23 – 25)

Tomb 24: Tomb missing: HEBRAND

Tomb 25: (THNOC 291) Tomb missing: LESPRIT. This tomb has been removed since the THNOC survey.

Tomb 26: (THNOC 292) Tomb missing: DERBIGNY . This tomb has been removed since the THNOC survey.

Ici Repose
Julien Naba
Ne en Afrique
Decede le 11 Juin 1839, age de 60 ans

Melite Verret

Vve Julien Naba
Decedee le 25 Avril 1853, a l'age de 102 ans.
Ah si nos veaux (vieux?) pouvaient (se) faise entendre
Si nous soupins (soupirs?) j'animaient (__) oevelne
(__) gai de saprue (__)

(If our old could be heard
If we sigh (?) animated
Cheerful and (?))

Note: The NAACP pamphlet calls this "one of the rarest monuments of
Afro-American history," due to its marble stone dedicated to an African
man who died as early as 1839. Sadly, the plaque is no longer present.

Tomb 27: (THNOC 293) BAKEWELL; Dumeny (alternate spellings
Duminy and Duminie)

Ici Repose
Louise Ducloslance
Epouse de Ducloslance
Nee 1 Juin 1808
Decedee 1 Avril 1839

Tomb 28: (THNOC 294) SIMON; Thomas

J. J. Simon
1900 – 1919

Willie Davina
Died February 26, 1937

Mrs. Antonia Thomas
Died April 7, 1951

Henry Eustis
Louisiana
CPL HQ CO 801 Pioneer Inf
March 26 1890 – July 5 1966

A. Thomas

Gary W. Johnson
(Aug) 1800 – Dec 1980

Joseph Millon, Jr.
US Navy
1921 - 1991

Tomb 29: (THNOC 295) HAYDEL; RIVARDE; FARR; GLORENS; McKendall

Ici Reposent
Angelique Eugenie Rivarde
Nee en cette ville
Decedee le Octobre 1836
Agee de 24 ans

P. B. Bernoville
Decede le 10 Mars 1857
Age 54 ans

Dame Seraphine Haydel
Decedee le 20 Aout 1860
Agee de 68 ans

In memory of
Florence Farr
Died December 12, 1954, age 68 years

Discrepancies
Row D: St. Philomene's Aisle

The spreadsheet puts Leola Marie Burke in Tomb 2; map has Burke in Tomb 1; THNOC shows Leola Marie Burke in Tomb 1. It's possible that the long list of names under Tomb 1 in the spreadsheet are from the Society Tomb next door.

The spreadsheet puts Labat and Benoit in Tomb 11, which the map and THNOC agree are in Tomb 12. The spreadsheet puts " Rousseau et Thezan" in Tomb 12, which the map and THNOC agree are in Tomb 15.

Spreadsheet shows Verret at Tomb 14 (which is missing in THNOC). The THNOC information shows Melite Verret along with Julien Naba at Tomb 26 (THNOC 292). Since both tombs are missing, it's hard to know which information is correct. The map in the NAACP pamphlet supports Tomb 26 as the correct site.

Tombs 25 (THNOC 291) and 26 (THNOC 292) have been crossed off on the SOC map, but are on the THNOC with numbers. They must have been removed between 1981 and 2009.

Tomb 29 is on the SOC map at St. James's Aisle, Row SL, Tomb 14.

ROW E
St. Philomene's Aisle (Alley No. 1 - L), Right

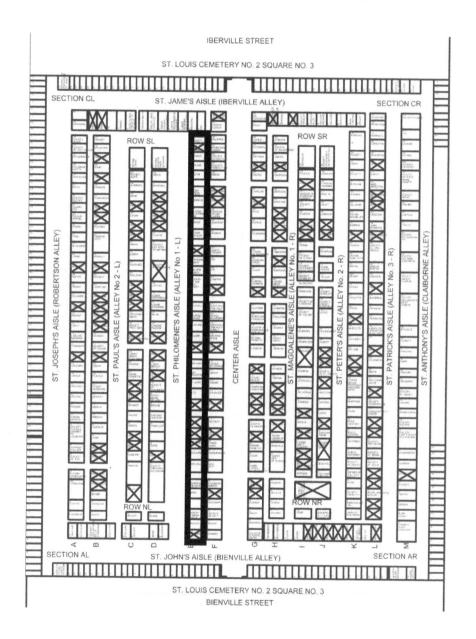

Row E: St. Philomene's Aisle (Alley No 1 - L)
Right Side

THNOC numbers 247 – 273

The tombs are counted as we're walking away from Bienville and toward Iberville, with Robertson to our left and Claiborne to our right.

Tomb 1: Tomb missing: probably GARDEVICILLE

Tomb 2: (THNOC 273) BACCHUS (George)

Ci Git

Shannon Augistin Bacchus
Decedee le 22 Avril 1858
A l'age de 36 ans

Leonine O. Bacchus
Decedee le 10 Oct 1882
A l'age de 22 ans

George Bacchus
Decedee le 7 Mai 1890
A l'age de 22 ans.
Ci-gisent

Joseph Pierre
Decedee le 14 Fev 1849
Age d'environ 69 ans.

H. Marie Simeonc
Decedee le 22 Janv 1850
A l'age de 19 ans

Claire Franc. Pierre
Decedee le 10 Dec 1850
A l'age de 67 ans

V. Jacques Bacchus
Decedee le 22 Sept 1854
A l'age de 50 ans

Tomb 3: (THNOC 272) SOCIETY OF MEN'S VIDALIA; Beaulieu (E.);
Brown (Chas); Davis (J.); Honore (J.P.); Liston (D.H.); Marigny (Edgar);
Pinkney (T.L.); Poree (Thomas); Whaley (H.A.)

Young Men's Vidalia B.A. Jrs.
Organized September 16, 1886

Incorporated July 22, 1889
Erected October 23, 1892

In Memoriam
Thomas Poret
T.C. Pinkley
J.P. Honore
Edgar Marigny
J. Davis
Chas Brown
E. Beaulieu
D.H. Liston
H.A. Whaley

Tomb 4: (THNOC 271) No name

Tomb 5: (THNOC 270) JORDE (alternate spelling Jorda); Bernard (Felice M.)

In memory of a Christian soul
Felicie M. Bernard
Born ??
30th date 1880 died 5th (M?)
Remembered by family
God-bless-her-we-pray-God-will-keep-her-amen

Tomb 6: (THNOC 269) SISTERS OF THE HOLY FAMILY

In pious remembrance of our beloved **Rev Mother M. Austin, born Jones**
(Ge)neral Superioress of the Sisters of the Holy Family
Died February 12, 1909, in the 48th year of her age
And the 32nd year of religion

Mother Mary Ursula Mollot
Died February 15, 1900, in the 43rd year of her age
And the 20th year of religion

Sister Mary Ann Fazende
Born ( ) died Feby 5, 1919
Aged (?) years (?) mos 24 days
(?) religion 69 yrs
R.I.P.

Note: At the time of the Tablet Survey, a detached tablet was leaning against this tomb, which they speculated came from the tomb's upper vault. This tablet was gone by 2016.

Tomb 7: (THNOC 268) LANEUVILLE (alternate spellings Doleolle, Doliolle, Laneville, Lanenville) (Dorothea)

Dorothea Laneuville

Tomb 8: (THNOC 267) AGUILLARD (alternate spelling Aquillard) (Alphonse A., Sr.); Boisdoir (alternate spelling Boisidore).

Alphonse A. Aguillard Sr
PFC 4095 O M Service Co, World War II
July 17, 1917 – May 14, 1969

My dear husband
J. L. Bonnot
Died October 13, 1928

I D A Bonnot
Died September 19, 1929
Our **Lia Dominique**
Born March 1, 1898; died March 16, 1925

Tomb 9: Tomb missing: MCCARTY

(Photo includes missing Tombs 9 – 12).

Tomb 10: Tomb missing: POREE; VICTOR

Tomb 11: Tomb missing: PERCY

Tomb 12: Tomb missing: REINE

Tomb 13: (THNOC 266) VILTZ (alternate spelling Veltz, Vilitz) (James); Gray (Louis V., Melvin); Pembrooks (Nathan); Peralta; Sabatier (Lillian P.); Smith (Thema W.); Thilboult (Elouise D.); Torregan (Planthia); Washington (Dorothy "Sally")

In memory of
Our Loved Ones
James Veltz
Died January 30, 1927

Nathan Pembrooks
Died June 25, 1954

My dear wife
Dorothy "Sally" Washington
Died October 1, 1956

Thelma W. Smith
June 2, 1961

Dianthia T. Torregano
December 5, 1962

Lillian P. Sabatier
Born November 27, 1898; died September 17, 1968

Elouise D. Thiboult
April 30, 1971

Louise V. Gray
June 9, 1976

Melvin Gray
1967 – 1996

Evelyn Elouise Gray
November 16, 1935 – May 4, 2013

THNOC note: "The inscription which follows was found on the reverse side of the closure tablet after a recent burial. Though the names thereon inscribed appear at this location this does not definitely indicate that these people are interned in this tomb." By this, they really mean on the reverse of the tablet, not the tomb itself, so there is no visible indication of this.

Sacred
Rose Chouteau
Nee a la N.elle Orleans
Decedee le 21 Mars 1846
Agee de 100 ans

M.me V.ve Legrod
Morte le 13 Mars 1859
A l'age de 68 ans

Ann Peralt
Morte le 27 Mai 1861
A l'age de 17 ans

M.me Vau Joseph Decat (V.ve)
Decedee le 10 Octobre 1882
A l'age de 72 ans

Tomb 14: (THNOC 265) WILLIAMS (Anita)

In memory of my wife
Anita M. Williams
February 1, 1898 – December 17, 1972

Arthur Castaino (Castaing?)
Died August 30, 1877
Aged 32 years

M.me Aime Martin
Died December 20, 1887
Aged 70 years

Note: A tablet was leaning against the tomb at the time of the THNOC survey. It is no longer there.

Tomb 15: (THNOC 264) LABAT (alternate spelling Labt) (Casimir, Olivia Martin); GRANDPRE; Chaodurier

Casimir Labat
Beloved husband of

Olivia Martin Labat
June 10, 1871 – June 6, 1941

A detached tablet is leaning on the ledge, as of 2016:

My Dear Husband
Anthony Grandpre
January 17, 1983 – May 23, 1950

Tomb 16: (THNOC 263) GASPARD Octave); Dupre; Tio

Gaspard

F. W.

Octave Okie Gaspard
Born May 1, 1895 – Died June 8, 1983

Tomb 17: Tomb missing: COUSIN

Note: The NAACP pamphlet identified this missing tomb as the resting place of writer Joanni Questy. Born in 1818, he was a celebrated poet and novelist, who Desdunes called "a refined scholar" and "one of the most learned men of his time" (25).

Tomb 18: (THNOC 262) STAURIN; Lavigne

Marie Anne Chalamber
July 1848

Tomb 19: (THNOC 261) BEAULIED (alternate spelling Beaulieu);
Staurin (Marie Lavines)

Ici Repose
(Jean) Louis (Be(?)ulle(t))

Marie Lovine Staurin
Born November 1, 1861; died March 28 1922

Note: The plaque set on the bricks reads "Staurin." This was possibly moved from Tomb 18 (THNOC 262).

Tomb 20: (THNOC 260) JOLIBOIS (Jean); AUGUST; Francois (M. Denege); Harden (Ouida)

Jolibois – August

Harden

Ouida A. Harden
March 16, 1904 – Oct. 26, 1998

Tomb 21: (THNOC 259) MITCHELL (Eleanor); Jolibois

Eleanor G. Mitchell
Died November 28, 1962

Tomb 22: (THNOC 258) SISTERS OF THE HOLY FAMILY;
Birmingham (Mother Mary Eusebia); Mother Mary Elizabeth; Goodman
(Mother Mary Philip); Hypolite (Eugene, Eugene (widow); Eulalie

Sisters of the Holy Family

Here lie the remains of **Eugene Hypolite**
Died October 25, 1894, aged 77 years

Widow of Eugene Hypolite
Died April 25, 1895, aged 78 years

Eulalie Hypolite
Died October 20, 1933, aged 90 years

Mother Mary Eusebia Birmingham
1876 – 1947
Superioress
1924 – 1927

To the memory of
Mother Mary Elizabeth
Superioress, Sisters of the Holy Family
1909 – 1918 and 1930 – 1946
Born November 26, 1874; died March 9, 1948
We have loved her in life
Let us not forget her in death

Mother Mary Philip Goodman
1885 – 1960
Superioress
1946 – 1958
RIP

Tomb 23: (THNOC 257) SOCIETY SAINTE CLOTILDE (alternate spelling Society of Soclotilde)

Societe Sainte Clotilde
Fondee le 16 Oct 1864
Incorporee le 4 Juin 1872

Tomb 24: (THNOC 256) GUIGESSE, LONGY (alternate spelling Longny, Longer, Long)

Tombeau de la Famille Robin De Longry

Tomb 25: Tomb missing: Bogengy

Tomb 26: (THNOC 255) PICHON, POPULUS

Tomb 27: Tomb missing: DUPUIS

Note: This tomb was present at the time of the THNOC survey, which said it was "blank, deteriorated, vault closures gone," along with "cracked" and "deteriorated." It was not on the SOC survey, so must have been removed before then.

Tomb 28: (THNOC 254) LA ROSE MYSTERIEUSE

La Rose Mysterieuse
Fondee le 21 Octobre 1860

Tomb 29: (THNOC 253) DUBREUIL (Mrs. H. O.); Glaudin

Mrs. H.O. Dubreuil is listed in THNOC 252; see Discrepancies.

Tomb 30: (THNOC 252) ROBIN; SIMON (Eva Fouche); MARINE (Leon, Wm. J., Wm. V. Jr.); Ballon (Jerome W.); Dupre (Daniel A.); Robin

Eva B. Haydel
Born August 29, 1903; died April 8, 1926

Mrs. H. O. Dubreuil
Died September 11, 1928, age 78 yreas

Robin – Simon – Marine

Wm. J. Marine
Aug. 9, 1874 – April 8, 1945

Leon M. Marine
May 17, 1920 – May 11, 1947

Wm. V. Marine, Jr.
Mar. 9, 1938 – Nov. 21, 1968

Jerome W. Ballon
Born May 11, 1919; died August 15, 1919

Eva Fouche Simon
Born June 6, 1893; died August 22, 1921

Daniel A. Dupre
September 12, 1937 – October 2, 1938

Tomb 31: (THNOC 251) BARZON (alternate spelling Bazon) (D'Aunoy, Henry, Lawrence); Annoy (alternate spelling D'Aunoy?) (Lester); Mansion (Lumen ?) (sic); Populus (Achille, Florice); Proctor; Trevigne (Josephine)

Henry Barzon
US Army
World War I
July 9, 1888 – February 1, 1978

Achille Lucien Populus
Died May 4, 1929, aged 69 years

Florice Populus
Born September 12, 1861; died Dec 28, 1948, age 87 yrs

Josephine Trevigne
Born March 27, 1853; died April 18, 1951

Lumena L.C. Mansion
Born March 6, 1885; died June 19, 1967

Lawrence Barzon
Born September 3, 1924; died November 10 1979

Blanche L. D'Auncy Barzon
Born February 28, 1891; died December 10, 1987

Tomb 32: (THNOC 250) BREAUX (Clementine, Theriot); Dupin; Martinez (Bessie E.); Nelder (Edward Jr.); Porche (Lionel A.)

Breaux Family

Clementine Breaux
Died July 11, 1930

Theriot Breaux
Died June 29, 1933

Lionel A. Porche
Died January 28, 1956

Edward Nelder, Jr.
Died September 30 1934, age 21 years

Bessie E. Martin
Died April 20, 1942

Tomb 33: (THNOC 249) JENKINS

Tomb 34: (THNOC 248) Tomb missing: WALLE; LAMBERT. This tomb has been removed since the THNOC survey.

Tablet leaning on back of tomb:

Mll Sophie Manuel
Decedee 10 Avril 1831, age de 60 ans
(___) fils

Francois Manuel

Tomb 35: (THNOC 247) SOCIETY OF ST. FELICITE

Jeanrette Lambert, 1889

Discrepancies
Row E: St. Philomene's Aisle

In this row, we're off count right off the bat. On the map, the first tomb in the row is crossed off, and it's listed as St. John's Aisle, Row NL, Tomb 5. Then the count of tomb starts with Bacchus. I'm counting that missing tomb as Tomb 1, so the tombs in this entire row will be one ahead of the map and the spreadsheet.

Tomb 27: This is labeled "Dupuis" on the SOC map and spreadsheet, but it was uncounted, and treated as a missing tomb, in the THNOC survey. The original handwritten SOC map also shows an unlabeled space.

Tomb 29 (THNOC 253): The SOC spreadsheet shows Dubreuil in this tomb. However, the THNOC information shows the same person in Tomb 30 (THNOC 252), which has a new stone reading "Robin – Simon – Marine."

Tomb 34 (THNOC 248): Numbered in THNOC survey, but crossed off on SOC map. The tomb itself is missing.

ROW F
St. Louis Aisle (Center Aisle), Left

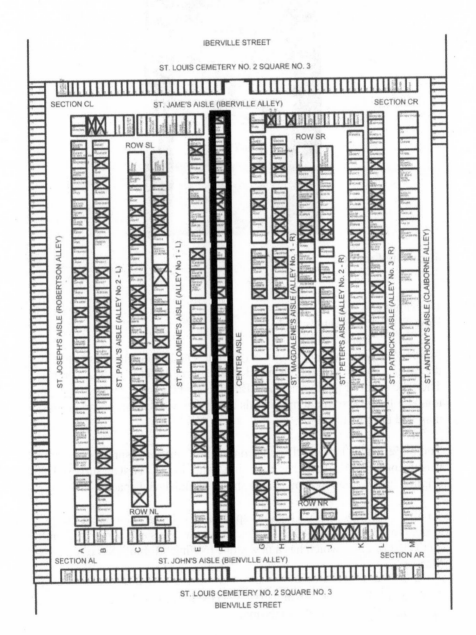

Row F: St. Louis Aisle (Center Aisle)
Left Side

THNOC numbers 208 – 237

The tombs are counted as we're walking away from Bienville and toward Iberville, with Robertson to our left and Claiborne to our right.

Tomb 1: (THNOC 208) ROBERT (Louise, Rene); Sindos

Louise Dannel Robert

Rene Robert

Note: This tomb is flat on the ground.

Tomb 2: (THNOC 209) MOORE (E.J., Gason); Delorme (altenate spelling Delarue)

E. J. Moore
Born August 1, 1838; died October 1, 1898

Gaston F. Moore, Jr.
Born September 6, 1916; died September 8, 2006

C. J. Moore
Born October 4, 1944; died November 11, 2010

Bernardine Bart Moore
Born December 12, 1920; died September 3, 2011

Tomb 3: (THNOC 210) SOCIETY of Dames Del; Williams (Gertrude)

Gertrude Williams
Died December 22, 1905

Tomb 4: (THNOC 211) Lalonier (alternate spelling CALONIER); Enfants; St. Aug

Famille F. Lalonier

Tomb 5: Tomb missing: CAVALIER

Tomb 6: (THNOC 212) LADIES OF MERCY (alternate name Society of Dames Mercy); Brightman (S.); Jackson (F.); Marshall (L.); Richard (C., Josephine); Smith (L.); Southall (Chad J., L.)

Ladies of Mercy B M A A
Organized September 14, 1902
Incorporated April 29, 1903

Officers
Josephine Richard, Pres
L. Southall Vice Pres
Chas J. Southart, Sec
C. Richard, Treas

L. Marshall Coll R
S. Brightman Chr. Re. Comm.
L. Smith 1.st Com
F. Jackson, 2.nd Com

Tomb 7: (THNOC 213) SLIE (alternate spelling Sly) (Nelva Rey, Waldo J. Jr., Waldo J. Sr.); REY (alternate spelling Ray) (Josephine, Hippolye J., Marguerite Blanc, Wilhelmine de Lay, Willis); Blanchard

Slie – Rey

Josephine Rey nee Blanchard
July 31, 1870 – November 22, 1853

Wilhelmine DeLay Rey
December 8, 1918 – October 4, 1982

Waldo J. Slie, Jr.
October 21, 1914 – December 21, 1982

Hippolyte J. Rey
December 12, 1906 – January 6, 1984

Nelva Rey Slie
January 25, 1913 – March 7, 1984

Marguerite Blanc Rey
August 2, 1911 – April 1, 1999

Willis Rey
January 29, 1911 – November 6, 2011

Waldo J. Slie, Jr.
December 11, 1939 – August 24, 2004

Fred Caliste
July 4, 1934 – October 19, 2014

Tomb 8: (THNOC 214) GORDEVIOLS (alternate spellings Cordeviolle, Cordevoile, Corderiole) (Marie); Famille Paul Commagere; White (Yvonne)

Famille Paul Commagere

Ici reposent
Marie Cordeviolle
Decedee le 28 Dec 1825
A l'age de 35 ans
Et sa fille

Dame Paul Commagere
Nee Eugenie Commagere
Decedee le 15 Aout 1879
A l'age de 62 ans
Yvonne M. White
1939 – 1963

Tomb 9: (THNOC 215) WARD; LANG (alternate spelling Lane); Hall (James H.)

Ward and Lang Family Tomb

James H. Hall
WOJG US Army
June 2, 1919 – July 4, 1974

Tomb 10: Tomb missing: SOCIETY of St. Augustine

Tomb 11: (THNOC 216) SOCIETY of St. Ignace

Ladies St Ignace No 3

Tomb 12: Tomb missing: LIONTAUD (alternate spelling Lioutaud); Cavalier

Tomb 13: (THNOC 217) CAVALIER

Cavalier

Tomb 14: (THNOC 218) ADAMS (David, Eleanora, George A., Herman, Vivian); Bacchus; Jefferson (Albert J., Sr.)

Adams

George A. Adams
1884 – 1974

Eleanora Adams
1891 – 1973

1912 **David** 1925

1918 **Herman** 1927

1924 **Vivian** 1951

Ci Git
Henry Hopkins
Ne le 4 Decembre 1800
Mort le 14 Novembre 1826

Ci-git aussi
Theodorine Segond
Nee le 1(4) Juillet 1830
Decedee le 2 Octobre 1839

Pierre Posthil
Decede le 4 Mars 1850
A l'age de 44 ans

Tomb 15: (THNOC 219) HARDY (Peter P.); Ford (Mercedes); Hopkins

In memory of our dear mother
Mercedes Ford +
Born August 24, 1903; died January 26, 1963

Father
Peter R. Hardy
Born November 22, 1901; died August 5, 1964

James Morning, Jr.
November 1, 1942 – December 10, 1976

Nira H. Boudy
August 24, 1934 – June 25, 1988

Mildred H. Morning
February 4, 1922 – August 31, 1997

De'Angelo Jules Hardy
June 18, 1984 – February 6, 2001

Ci Git
Marie Louise Dominique
Fille de Fanchon Dupart
Epouse de Jean Baptiste Hardy
J.B. Hardy
Decedee le 15 Avril 1827
(a l'age) de 48 ans

Tomb 16: (THNOC 220) LADIES ST. IGNACE (alternate name Society of St. Ignace); Dupart

Ladies St. Ignace No. 2

Note: At the time of the Table Survey, two pieces of tablet were leaning against this tomb that fit Tomb 19 (THNOC 222). They were gone by 2016. They read: 17 Nov 1844, de 49 ans.

Tomb 17: Tomb missing: DAUPHIN; Cook (William)

Tomb 18: (THNOC 221) MEYERS (alternate spelling Meyer); COOK; Dale (Marie Bejamine (?)) (sic); Sisters of Holy Family

Mrs. Jennie Myers
Died May 19, 1924

William Cook
Died September 24, 1944

Note: This tomb is flat, with a frame on the ground, filled with crushed stones.

Tomb 19: (THNOC 222) SISTERS OF THE HOLY FAMILY; Bourgeois (Laura R.); Hazeur; Rivoli (Rock); Rousseau

Ici Repose
Marie Benjamin Dale
Epouse de Teophile Hazeur
Denoier (sic) le 15 De(c) 1844

Florville (marble-cutter)

Note: A much older stone with this same information became detached, and must have been replaced. As of 2014, it was leaning in Row I, between tombs 11 and 12.

Tomb 20: (THNOC 223) RIVOLI; BOURGEOIS; Garcia

Ici reposent
Manuel Garcia
Decede le 28 Mai 1828
A l'age de 51 ans

(?) Garcia
(?) le Juin (?) 1837
A l'age de 17 ans

(?) de la Vincendiere
(?) Octobre 1866

(?) Coralie Gardly
(?) Juillet 1870
Florville

Rock Rivoli
June 7, 1921 – Oct. 11, 1987

Laura R. Bourgeois
Aug. 22, 1914 – Oct. 21, 2000

Tomb 21: (THNOC 224) SISTERS OF THE HOLY FAMILY; Charles (Josephine); Delille (Henriette, Founderess of the Sisters of the Holy Family) (alternate name Harriette Delsle); Gaudin (Juliette); Society of Holy Grail

Sisters of the Holy Family

Mere Henriette Delille
1813 – 1862
Fondatrice de La Maison de la Ste. Famille, Et La Premiere Superieure
(Founder of the house of the Holy Family, and the First Superior).

Mother Josephine Charles
1812 – 1885
Third Superior

Mother Juliette Gaudin
1808 – 1888
Cofoundress and Second Superior

To the memory of Mother Mary of the Sacred Heart
Eight Superioress of the Sisters of the Holy Family
1918 – 1924
Born January 23, 1861; died June 4, 1933
RIP

Note: The THNOC information shows her as "Mere Harriette." Henriette Delille founded the Sisters of the Holy Family in 1842, along with co-founder Juliette Gaudin. Josephine Charles joined the order a year later. Delille died on November 17, 1862. A free woman of color, she dedicated herself to teaching and assisting the poor, including slaves, has been in the process of canonization since 1988. She was declared "Venerable" by Pope Benedict XVI in 2010. According to the NAACP pamphlet, "more than two hundred" women from the order are buried in Square 3, in three tombs. The others are in Row E, Tomb 6 (THNOC 269), and Row K, Tomb (THNOC 110).

Tomb 22: Tomb missing: SOCIETY of St. Coeur

Tomb 23: (THNOC 225) ZAMORA (alternate spelling Zamore); Bienvenu (Jules R.)

Tomb 24: (THNOC 226) Dauphin; Delaidt (Jr.)

Jules Bienvenu
P.F.C. U.S. Army
1908 - 1992

Tomb 25: (THNOC 227) Garcia

Ici Repose
Adelaide J. Tarascon
Decedee le 6 Decembre 1828
Agee de 70 ans

Tomb 26: (THNOC 228) JUSTIN (Joseph R. Sr., Sidney); THOMAS (alternate spelling Thompson?) (E. T., Prancelle (?) P.) (sic)

Al( ) de Liguory
( ) Dec 1875

Marcelle P. Thompson
June 27, 1943 - January 12, 2000

E.T. Thompson
November 16, 1942 - January 19, 2007

Sidney Justin
February 11, 1886 - December 29, 1968

Joseph R. Justin, Sr.
April 21, 1897 - November 13, 1970

Tomb 27: (THNOC 229) HAZEUR

Tomb 28: (THNOC 230) COUVENT (alternate spelling Couveint)
(Bernard, Marie C.)

M. Bernard Couvent
Native d'Afrique
Decedee le 29 Juin 1837
Agee denui lon 80 ans

Note: Madame Couvent, frequently cited as Marie, was named Justine
Fervin Couvent. She was the widow of Gabriel Bernard Couvent, and

probably a former slave (Desdunes 101). In her will, she endowed a school for "poor black Catholic orphans" (ibid). The school finally opened in 1848. After the Civil War, the school was largely abandoned, but was revived by a group of "patriotic and generous men" (107), Desdunes and his brother among them. Arthur Esteves (St. James's Aisle, Tomb 6, THNOC 33) is also on the list of supporters.

Tomb 29: (THNOC 231) LADIES AND YOUNG LADIES PERPETUAL HELP; Society of Louisiana

Ladies and Young Ladies Perpetual Help

Organized December 1, 1929

Cornerstone:
Officers
J. Santiago, Pres
C. Screau, Vic
Z. Dandrid, Rc. Sec
G. Gletcher, Fin Sec
J. Blandin, Tre
L. Villa, 1.st Com
H. Santiago, 2.nd Com
Finance Com
O. Davis, Fin Com
A. Mandadam Chair

Fragment leaning against tomb:

Ici reposent
Marie Cavalier
Morte le 15 Octobre
Agee de 25 ans

Et sa soeur
Marie
Epouse de
Joseph Brici
Morte le 24 ( ) 182( )
Agee de ( )
(Re)pose
( )assite
( )rs 1785
( ) 1829

Isnard (marble-cutter)

Tomb 30: Tomb missing; COURAND (alternate spelling Courano)

(Photo includes missing Tombs 30 – 31)

Tomb 31: Tomb missing; DEVERGIE (alternate spelling Deverges)

Tomb 32: (THNOC 232) KNOX (alternate spelling Know) (Emily Anthony); Laveaux (Alphonse); Raphael (Jullette Laveaux); Yosti (alternate spelling Yosthi, Yosthis) (Augustin)

Emile Anthony Knox
May 2, 1902 – August 20, 1976

In memory of my
Alphonse Laveaux
Born October 31, 1884; died October 1, 1951

To our beloved mother
Juliette Laveaux Raphael
Died May 15, 1948

Tomb 33: (THNOC 233) SOCIETY of VENUS STAR; C.J. Boisseau & Son Builders

(C) Officers
Benj Blanchard Pres
E. J. Brunet Ace
A. E. Saloy Rec Sect
C. Bathelemy Asst.
A. Leopold Ful
J. L. Pratts Treas

Tomb 34: (THNOC 234) SOCIETY LE EQUITE (alternate spelling Societe le Equile)

Tomb 35: (THNOC 235) SOCIETY OF REINE DE AUGES

Reine des Auges

Tomb 36: (THNOC 236) ALLIANCE Society; Alexander (Mary)
(alternate spelling Allnander)

Mary (＿)nander
(＿) 1902
Note: THNOC transcribed as Allnander; probably Alexander.

Tomb 37: (THNOC 237) LABAUD (alternate spelling Labeau, Labeaux); LAVILLE (Marie Louise)

Cit-git
Marie Louise Laville
Nee en cette Paroisse
(Born in this parish)
Decedee le 21 Janvier 1837
Agee de 80 ans
Bonne mere et bonne amie est regrettee
De ses enfants et de tout ceux qui l'out connu.
(A good mother and a good friend regretted by her children and all who knew her)

Tomb 38: Tomb missing; names CABARET, Jourdain (alternate spelling Jourdan)

Discrepancies
Row F: St. Louis Aisle

Tomb 12: This is showing as missing and uncounted in the THNOC survey, but the handwritten SOC map shows Liontaud. The updated SOC map has it crossed off, and the spreadsheet gives the names Liontaud and Cavalier (which may be where a spreadsheet glitch crept in; see next tomb).

Tomb 13 (THNOC 217): the SOC spreadsheet diverges from the map here. Both show Cavalier, but the spreadsheet adds a list of Adamses. Then the spreadsheet shows Tomb 14 (THNOC 218) as Adasm, with a list of Hardys included, and Tomb 15 (THNOC 219) also as Hardy. The maps and visual verification agree that Tomb 13 is Cavalier, Tomb 14 is Adams, and Tomb 15 is Hardy.

The map and the spreadsheet are back in sync by Tomb 16 (THNOC 220).

Tomb 23 (THNOC 225): the SOC spreadsheet shows Jules R. Bienvenu in this tomb. However, the THNOC information puts him in Tomb 24 (THNOC 226).

The updated SOC maps shows Tomb 24 (THNOC 226) and Tomb 25 (THNOC 227) as "??" The handwritten SOC map and the spreadsheet show "Dauphin" and "Garcia."

ROW G
St. Louis Aisle (Center Aisle), Right

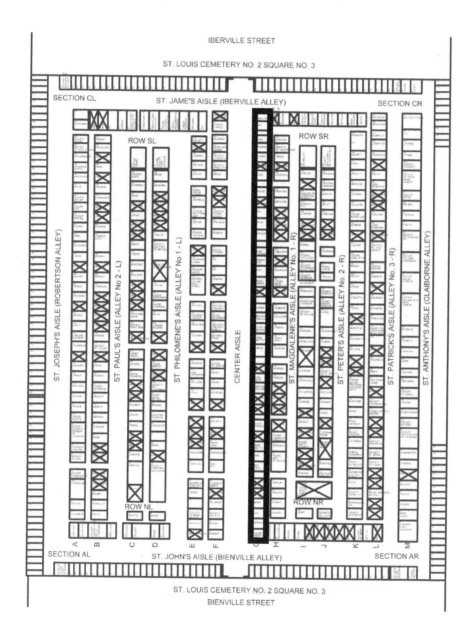

Row G: St. Louis Aisle (Center Aisle)
Right Side

THNOC numbers 1 – 30

The tombs are counted as we're walking away from Bienville and toward Iberville, with Robertson to our left and Claiborne to our right.

Tomb 1: (THNOC 1) DALCOUR; COURCELLE; WHITE

Ici Repose
Delphine Dalcour
Epouse de Mirtille Courcelle

Mirtelle Courcelle
Decedee le 13 Fev 1872
A l'age de 72 ans

Barbara F. White
Born July 30, 1938; died October 19, 1967

Florville (marble-cutter)

Note: According to the NAACP pamphlet, Mirtille Courcelle, born in 1800, was a wealthy businessman at the time of the Civil War.

Tomb 2: (THNOC 2) MONTPLAISIR; Thomas

Montplaisir Family

Tomb 3: (THNOC 3) SALOY

A. E. Saloy
Died March 6, 1924 aged 52 yrs.

Tomb 4: (THNOC 4) ALBRIERS (alternate name Albrier)

Ici Repose
Mademoiselle Caroline Albriers
Nee a la Nell Orleans
Decedee le 3 Dbre 1829
A l'age de 54 ans
Elle emporte (__)elle-les
regrette de sa famille
 et de ceux qui (l'amment)
lendrement.
(Regretted by her family and all who loved her tenderly)

Tomb 5: Tomb missing, PETIT

(Photo includes missing Tombs 5 – 6)

Tomb 6: Tomb missing, GRIFFIN; JOLLY (alternate spelling Jolyy)

Tomb 7: (THNOC 6) LADIES SOCIETY OF OLIVE BRANCH; Oscar James DUNN

Ladies Olive Branch

Oscar James Dunn
1826 – 1871
Lieutenant Governor of Louisiana 1868 – 1871
Grand Master Prince Hall of Louisiana Masons 1864-67

Note: Dunn is described in the NAACP pamphlet as "one of the most powerful and influential politicians of the Reconstruction Era." This plaque is on the side of the tomb:

Tomb 8: (THNOC 7) GODIN (alternate spelling Gaudin); Poree

Ici Git
(F)rancoise Gode(y)
Epouse de Charles Poree
Decedee le 21 Janier 1830 dans sa 16 annee
Par ses vertus elle fut chire
A son epouse et ses parens,
Mais maigre leurs gemissemens
Ellae toret petit sur le terr.
(For her virtures she was dear
to her husband and her parents,
but their meager groans
(??) small on the earth)

Tomb 9: (THNOC 8) **MEDINA; MONETTE;** Sindos

Monette Family

Medina-Monette

Tomb 10: Tomb missing, VIVIER (alternate spelling Vives)

Tomb 11: (THNOC 9) SOCIETY LA CANDEUR (alternate spelling Society of Londeur)

Society La Candeur

Note: According to the NAACP pamphlet, two of the children of P. B. S. Pinchback, who succeeded Oscar Dunn (Tomb 7 above) as Louisiana's Lieutenant Governor, are buried in this society tomb.

Tomb 12: Tomb missing, Manconi (alternate spelling Mainconi)

(Photo includes missing Tombs 12 – 13).

Tomb 13: Tomb missing, BRISTORE

Tomb 14: (THNOC 10) HARRISON; LABOSTRIE (alternate spelling Labostine)

This tomb is flat, with a frame on the ground, filled with crushed stones.

Harrison

La Bostrie

Tomb 15: (THNOC 11) YOUNG MEN OF ...; Lanna

Ici Repose
M.rie Horten(c)e Lanna
Nee le ( ) Avril 1(7)82
Decedee le 25 Aout 1830

Francois Valentin Pere
Mort a 61 ans.

Young Men of Liberty B.M.A.A.
Organized September (26, 1923)
Incorporated April (27, 1924)

Tomb Committee:
Wm. King Chr.
M. Nicholas
A. R. Hart
Jno. Holmes
Dedicated Apr 26, 1925

Officers:
P. R. Holmes Pres
W. Willis Vice
J. Holmes Rec. Sect.
G. Augustine Fin
W. M. Green Treas
J. W. Holmes Col

B. Williams G. Relief
E. Johnson 1. Finance
A. Pierre 1. Commis
F. Bailey 2.

Tomb 16: Tomb missing, JAMET

Tomb 17: (THNOC 12) LAURENT

Tomb 18: (THNOC 13) MEDINA; MONETTE; Daquin (alternate spelling D'Aquin, A'quin)

My Beloved Son
Will A. Dixon, Jr.
February 2, 1938 – December 13, 1964

My Beloved Husband
James Watts, Sr.
Died August 8, 1971, age 76 yrs.

Beloved Mother
Sadly missed by family
Anita D. Smith
1898 – 1990, age 91

Beloved Mother
Sadly missed by family
Clementine Duplessis
Born August 15, 1871; died May 4, 1959, age 87

James Roberts
1921 + 1977
Sadly missed
By family

Eva Duplessis
1906 – 1978
Sadly missed by family

Ethel Watts

1900 – 1991
Sadly missed by family

Velma Bonds
1924 – 1999

Shirley Taylor
1936 - 2004

Joseph Smith
Pvt US Army
World War I
October 9, 1897 - April 3, 1977

Tomb 19: (THNOC 14) SOCIETE DE BIENFAISANCE MUTUELLE;
Society of Les Amis Inseperables (alternate spelling Society of Amisinger)

Les Amis Inseperables Societe de Bienfaisance Mutuelle

Organisie le 15 Janvier 1878
Incorporated le 14 October 1878

O. Dumoiulle, Builder

Tomb 20: (THNOC 15) DUBUCLET (alternate spelling Oubuclet); GRANDJEAN

Famille Dubuclet

Assitha D. Grandjean
June 4, 1872 - July 25, 1945

Rene Grandjean
April 21, 1889 - May 10, 1986
Born in Vouzers Ardennes France

In Loving Memory of
Francois Dubuclet
August 10, 1837 - March 2, 1924

Note: according to the NAACP pamphlet, Antoine Dubuclet's family were prominent landowners before the Civil War, owning their own slaves, and Antoine served as the Louisiana State Treasurer from 1868 – 1879. Since the name "Grandjean" is associated with this tomb, it's likely that Rene Grandjean was also interred here. A Frenchman, and friend of Rodolphe Desdunes, he married Assitha Dubuclet on October 29, 1913 (in Jamaica, since they were an interracial couple). His collection of Dubuclet family records, correspondence with Desdunes, and records of séances and spiritualist activities are held in the University of New Orleans archives.

Tomb 21: (THNOC 16) CLAVERN; Brocard (Rosemond); Duplantier (Guy, Leona); Jeanbard (Elizabeth); LeBlanc (Isidore); McCarthy (Henry); Neat (George)

Ci-Git
Antoinette Claver
Nee le 19 Novembre
Et decedee le 3 nov. 1800

Ci-Git
(__) Claver
Decedee le 7 Avril 1831, age de 7 ans.

Tomb 22: Tomb missing, HARDY; POINCY

Tomb 23: (THNOC 17) DURPHY (alternate spelling Dupruy); LACRETE

Tomb 24: (THNOC 18) JUDOR (Judis)

Tomb 25: (THNOC 19) DUSSEAU (alternate spelling Dussuad, Dussuau); GIROD

The Dusseau Family (Emile)

In Memory of
Marietta Lundy
1925 – 1966

Pilicious DeLay
1895 - 1981

Tomb 26: (THNOC 20) YOUNG VETERANS; Society of Jr. B. A.

Plaque reads:

Ann J. Dejan and Leroy P. Lejan, Sr.
Restoration May 2015

Leaning tablet: **Famille S(a)(o)(d)t**

Tomb 27: (THNOC 21) DESARZANT (alternate spelling Dezargan)

Famille Desarzant

Antoine Desarzant

Henry Landry
Died January 26, 1834

Tomb 28: (THNOC 22) DUPUIS (alternate spelling Dupui, Duprex)

Familes Duffaut et Dupuis

Joseph Duffaut
Decedee le 19 Novembre 1899
A l'age de 67 ans

Aubertine Dupuis
Nee au Cap I.S.D. (Santa Dominguez?)
Decedee le 7 Sept. 1857
Agee de 67 ans

Ici repose
Urssule F. Dupuis

Tomb 29: (THNOC 23) ROSS

Ci Git
Matilde Gillet
De la Nouvelle Orleans
Decedee le 13 Janvier 1832 agee de 4 ans 2 mois

Tomb 30: Tomb missing, GILLET; LEFEBURE

Tomb 31: (THNOC 24) LABEAUD

Wm Labeaud

George L. Labeaud
Died June 7, 1931, age 22 years

Elva Gagnet
Died June 7, 1931, age 20 years

Alma Gagnet
Died June 7, 1931, age 25 years

Wm. L. Labeaud
Born July 13, 1885 – Died October 3, 1966

Vivian G. Labeaud
Born May 29, 1908 – Died April 6, 1974

William J. Labeaud
Born May 29, 1908 – Died April 6, 1974

Eva Labeaud
Born February 8, 1890 – Died August 2, 1985

Note: the story of George L. Labeaud, Elva Gagnet, and Alma Gagnet's deaths can be found on the CreoleGen website (www.creolegen.org), in a post called "Tragedy on Lake Pontchartrain- 1931." Their research includes several newspaper articles from the time. While wading in the lake during a picnic, several people were pulled into the lake by an undertow that was brought on by dredging. George Labeaud and Elva Gagnet were engaged, and Alma was Elva's sister. Three other friends also drowned in the incident, which many blamed on the lack of proper beach facilities for African-American residents.

Tomb 32: (THNOC 25) SELICO; Naba

In memory of
Bernice Selico
Born July 5, 1920; died April 22, 1945
Sadly missed by mother, sister, niece

Tomb 33: Tomb missing, BERTRAND

Tomb 34: (THNOC 26) RICHARD

Tomb 35: (THNOC 27) GUESNON; Soiresse; Tervalon

Famille Guesnon

Ici Repose
George Guesnon, Jr.
Nee Nov 24 1872 Decedee Fev 21 1935
A l'age de 63 ans.

You are loved
Eric David Guesnon
April 13, 1960 – January 6, 1977

Tomb 36: (THNOC 28) LADIES ST. IGNACE (alternate name Society of St. Ignace)

Ladies St. Ignace No. 1

Tomb 37: (THNOC 29) ROUD (alternate spelling Roup)

Ici repose
(Therene) Ro(u)(?)
Nee (?) le Jamiaque (Jamaica)
(?) 1801
Decedee le (13) Octobre (?)

Et
Irene Ro(u)t
Nee le (?)

Ici Repose

THNOC Note: "10 lines of inscriptions that cannot be read accurately due to thick layers of whitewash."

Tomb 38: (THNOC 30) Society of Ben Brothren (BB ASSOCIATES)

B. B. Association
Organized July 1864

Discrepancies
Row G: St. Louis Aisle

Tomb 5: Counted as tomb 5 in tablet survey; crossed off on map

Tomb 35: The name "Tervalon" is handwritten on the Carey map; transcribed with a typo on the SOC spreadsheet.

ROW H
St. Magdalene's Aisle (Alley No. 1 - R), Left

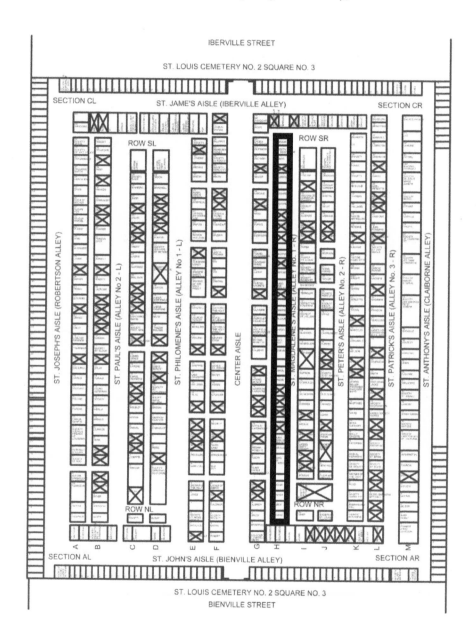

Row H: St. Magdalene's Aisle (Alley No. 1 -)
Left Side

THNOC numbers 39 – 62

The tombs are counted as we're walking away from Bienville and toward Iberville, with Robertson to our left and Claiborne to our right.

Tomb 1: (THNOC 62) ARCARD (alternate spelling Aicard)

Des enfants inconsolables ont erige ce (majore)
A la memoire de
(Her inconsolable children have erected this monument
To the memory of)
M.ie Henriette Bouchardeau
Nee au Port au Prince, ile d'Haiti:
Decedee le 18 Mai 1841
A l'age de 45 ans

Cette meme tombe renferme aussi san flls
(This same tomb also contains her son)
Drausin Dubois
Decedee le 7 Juillet 1834
A l'age de 18 ans

Carmelite R. Alcard
Decedee le 10 Dec, 1871, a l'age de 24 ans.

Tomb 2: (THNOC 61) VIGNES (L. A.); Montplaisir Family

Famille L. A. Vignes

Tomb 3: (THNOC 60) BRAZIER; Vandange

Societe de (--) de M.lle Selle
Tomb de St.(--)
Fonde le Dixhuit Janvier 1876

Tomb 4: (THNOC 59) HAZEUR; Crocker; Bazile

Memorial of
Mrs. Elvira Allen
Born April 3, 1928
Died May 13, 1959

Note: From the NAACP pamphlet: Bazile Crocker (1800 – 1879) was a noted swordsman, who ran a famous fencing academy, with both black and white students.

Tomb 5: (THNOC 58) Society of Victoire; YOUNG MEN OF ST. MICHAEL

At the time of the Tablet Survey, there was a stone leaning against Tomb 5 (THNOC 58). It was no longer there by 2014.

Ici repose
M. Eulalie Blai
Epouse de J. J. Montfort
Morte le 6 Nov 1845
A l'age de 39 ans
Elle laisse
Pour pleurer sa mort premature
Son epoux et ses trois enfans
(She leaves her husband and her three children to mourn her premature death)

Marie Blaisine Montfort
Mort le 15 Mars 1878

Florville

Tomb 6: (THNOC 57) Famille BOGUILLE (alternate spelling Boquille)

Famille Boguille

THNOC note: the rest of the tomb is completely smashed in.

Tomb 7: (THNOC 56) YOUNG LADIES OF CHARITY

Young Ladies of Charity B.M.A.A.
Organized February 5, 1899
Incorporated August 23, 1899

Officers
Josephine Richard, President
Corinne Bundy, V. President
C. J. Southall, Secty.
C. Richard, Treas.
Lucild Marshall, Coll.
Theresa Varisse, Chairlady R. C.
Alice McDonald, 1 Commissary
Elodie Jon, 2. Commissary

C. Richard
(?) Southall
(?) Jackson
Elizabeth Gregor
Rose Green
Pauline Fryer
Clothilde Etemen

Tomb 8: Tomb missing, LACLOTTE

(Photo includes missing Tombs 8 – 11).

Tomb 9: Tomb missing, GARDEVIER (Garnier, Garderes)

Tomb 10: Tomb missing, SOUVENIR

Tomb 11: Tomb missing, ROUX

Tomb 12: (THNOC 55) DUNCAN; Campanel; Conrad (Fred, Lt. F.); Duncan; Mornay (Louise); Nogess   (Irene Thiel); Thiel (Alfred G., Jr., George, Odeta E.)

Campanel

Tomb 13: (THNOC 54) BARRON; Cileval (Rosalie); Garron (alternate spelling Garon); Guillaume (Celestine)

(L)al(ie) (Eulalie)
Epouse de D.evil Barjon (sic)
Morte le 10 Fevrier 1836
A l'age de 34 ans
... larme passant sur la tombe d'Eulalie
Car si tu l'as connue tu as du l'almer.
(... passing the tomb of Eulalie
For if you knew of -- ??)

Monsseaux (stone-cutter)

Tomb 14: (THNOC 53) LASVEUR (alternate spelling LaSiuer); Freditt (Francoise); Lombard, Herbert, Manuel); Mach (Ray, Roy); Masters (Henry, Joseph, Olivia); Roche (Ralph)

Ici reposent
Leonide Mersebon
Decedee le Juillet 18(3?)
A la'ge de (41) ans

(----) Leonine
(---)

D(--) Miss Canflaneo
Decedee le (--) Mars 1860
A l'age de 80 ans

A. B. Ringold
Decedee le 9 Janvier 1871
A l'age de 72 ans

Dolord Merseron
Decedee le 30 Avril 1872
A l'age de 65 snd

Note: The name "Merceron" appears to have been more common in New Orleans, but there are also New Orleans Merserons listed in Ancestry.com.

Tomb 15: (THNOC 52) CONTY; DAGOT; Young Men's Moral

Tomb 16: (THNOC 51) CONRAD; Burrows (Evelyn D., Raymond G., Robert T., Jr., Robert T., Sr., Zelma M.); Colt (Earl S., Sr.); Evans (Leonard G.); Lautaud

A. F. Conrad

Fred Conrad
Born May 3, 1882; died October 25, 1934

Rev. A. F. Conrad
Died December 12, 1957

Louise Mornay
Born January 11, 1892 – Died January 9, 1962

George Thiel
Born January19, 1872; died June 20, 1933

Odeta E. Thiel
Born March 22, 1905; died October 15, 1987

Irene Thiel Nogess
Born March 8, 1920; died October 14, 1995

Alfred G. Thiel, Sr.
Born February 7, 1914; died July 15, 2000

Tomb 17: (THNOC 50) GUILLAUME; Cheval

Ici reposen
Celestine Guillaume
Decedee le 15 Janv 1835
Agee de 18 ans

Et sa mere
Rosalie Cheval
Decedee le 11 Sept 1810
Agee de 18 ans

Note: The cemetery was consecrated in 1823. Rosalie could have been moved to a new family tomb later. The dates or listed ages may have been read incorrectly, as Rosalie could not be Celestine's mother according to the above dates. If Celestine died in 1835 at the age of 18, she would have been born in 1817, after Rosalie's death.

Tomb 18: (THNOC 49) LOMBARD; Famille Broyard (alternate name Bayard)

Henry Masters, Sr.
Died July 4, 1949

Manuel C. Lombard
Died March 30, 1963

Joseph Masters
Died December 24, 1965

Herbert M. Lombard
Died January 9, 1966

Olivia T. Masters
1893 – 1979

Raphael Roche
Decedee le 7 Dec 1840
A l'age de 60 ans

Francoise
Epouse de Raphael Roche
Decedee le 22 Mai 1864
A l'age de 93 ans

Roy J. Mack, Sr.
1923 – 1998

Ray A. Mack

1957 - 2004

Tomb 19: (THNOC 48) Tomb missing, Leo Anthony Frank, LACHAISE

Note: This tomb was still there at the time of the THNOC survey, with a tablet leaning against the tomb. This tablet was no longer at this location by 2014.

Ici repose
Jeanne Depassau
Epouse de Louis Cavalier
Nee le 5 Fevrier 1815
Morte le 20 Fevrier 1837

M. Albertine Lorreins
Epouse de Louis Cavalier
Morte le 20 Mai 1860, a l'age de 36 ans

Isnard (marble-cutter)

Tomb 20: (THNOC 47) YOUNG MEN'S MORALITY (alternate name Society of Morality)

Young Men's Morality B.M.A.A.

Tomb Commander
Henry B. A. ( )
Ex officio
Jas N. ( )
Ex officio
George Robinson
L.N. Dej( )
F. L. Genmouny
Jos. J. Burns
Ernest Burns
V.L. Haroy
Jules Fo( )
J. M. ( )
Assistant Secretary
Assistant Secretary
George Robinson, Treasurer

Tomb 21: (THNOC 46) BURROWS; Harris (Alton Gilbert Sr.); Nelson (Auguste)

Burrows Family
In loving memory

Father
Robert Burrows, Sr.
November 22, 1900 – January 1, 1954

Mother
Evelyn D. Burrows
September 21, 1901 – March 28, 1989

Zelma M. Burrows
February 11, 1910 – February 24, 1984

Leonard Evans
March 9, 1938 - June 29, 1987

Raymond G. Burrows
September 16, 1931 – June 26, 1999

Robert T. Burrows, Jr.
September 11, 1925 – September 24, 1999

Earl S. Cole, Sr.
October 31, 1922 – January 21, 2001

Caden and Cylie McCullum
December 5, 2009   December 31, 2011
        May 14, 2015

Tomb 22: Tomb missing, TALHAND (alternate spelling Talhan)

Tomb 23: (THNOC 45) LABOSTRIE (alternate spelling Labosterie);
Armant (John Adolph, Viola Brewster); Gordon (Charles Louis)

B.mx Labostrie
(alias Valcon)

Tomb 24: Tomb is missing, Bordenave (Orelia); Tio

(Photo includes missing Tombs 24 – 26).

Tomb 25: Tomb is missing, Cupdion; alternate spelling Cupidon); Molosain

Tomb 26: Tomb is missing, Godoffe

Tomb 27: (THNOC 44) BROYARD

Famille Broyard

Ci-git

Catherine Godoffe
Nee au Cap Francais Ile St. Dque
Morte le 10 Feb 1817, agee de 70 ans.
Ses (__) pourcelles
(… for those)

Note: The cemetery was consecrated in 1823. It's possible that Catherine Godoffe was moved later into a newer family tomb.

Mme A. Bezou
Decedee le 25 Juillet 1892, a l'age de 50 ans.

Tomb 28: (THNOC 43) BROYARD (Tio); Wiltz

Elisabeth Alexis
Alias **Philosophe**
Nee a Jacmel L'ile d'Haiti 1783
Decedee le 18 Nov 1872

Note: This is almost certainly the tomb of a family described in the book *Louis Armstrong's New Orleans*, by Thomas Brothers. He says that Catalonian Marcos Tio owned a tavern on Decatur "in the 1790s," and had a family with a free woman of color named Victoire Wiltz; a descendant, jazz clarinet player Lorenzo Tio, Jr., was a contemporary of Armstrong's.

Tomb 29: (THNOC 42) COURSAULT

Tomb 30: Tomb missing, SINCERES

Note: The tomb was missing at the time of the Tablet Survey. It's possible that Sinceres was part of an Association name.

Tomb 31: (THNOC 41) HARRIS; Lainez

Harris

Auguste Nelson
Mort le 24 Decembre 1827, age de 21 ans

Note: His death date is listed as 12/21/1827 on the SOC spreadsheet.

Anton Gilbert Harris, Sr.
Pvt US Army
World War II
August 25, 1922 – September 18, 2006

Tomb 32: (THNOC 40) SOCIETY OF ST. MAGDALEINE (alternate
spelling Society of Sr Magdalenia)

Societe St. Magdelein

Tomb 33: (THNOC 39) GORDON; Armant

Charles Louis Gordon
PV2 US Army
December 12, 1964 – April 25, 1987

John Adolph Armant
September 21, 1879 – July 30, 1928

Viola Brewster Armant

November 21, 1884 – June 30, 1974

Discrepancies
Row H: St. Magdalene's Aisle

Tomb 24 and 25 are crossed off on the map, but included in the Tablet
Survey.

THNOC 48 = Numbered in THNOC survey, but crossed off on SOC map.
Tomb is missing as of 2014.

ROW I
St. Magdalene's Aisle (Alley No. 1 - R), Right

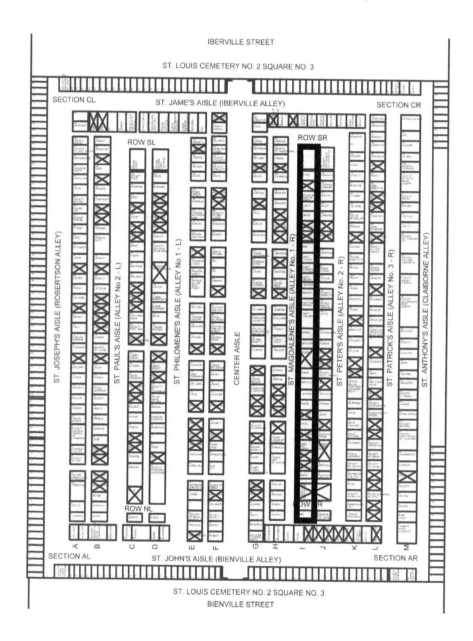

Row I: St. Magdalene's Aisle (Alley No. 1 - R)
Right Side

THNOC numbers 63 – 84

The tombs are counted as we're walking away from Bienville and toward Iberville, with Robertson to our left and Claiborne to our right.

Tomb 1: (THNOC 63) VINET

Famille P. Vinet

Tomb 2: Tomb is missing, SOCIETY OF CHRISTIAN DOCTRINE #1. The plot is big enough that it covers both Row I and Row J.

Tomb 3: (THNOC 64) ROBSON; Bellevue (alternate spelling Bellevoe)

Joseph Robson
Louisiana
Pvt Co C 4 Dev Bn
World War I
February 12, 1903 – January 1, 1961

Note: The Joseph Robson from New Orleans that can be found serving in World War I was born March 11, 1893, according to the database "U.S., World War I Draft Registration Cards, 1917-1918." If he had been born in 1903, he would have been 15 at the war's end.

Detached and leaning on 2nd vault:
( ) N Abie
1835

Tomb 4: Tomb is missing, SOCIETY OF ST. MARGUERITE

(Photo includes missing Tombs 4 – 5).

Tomb 5: Tomb is mising, CABALLE

Tomb 6: (THNOC 65) SOCITY OF UNITY CHARITY, (alternate name Ladies Unity Charity)

Ladies Unity Charity B.M.A.A.
Organized November 20, 1892; incorporated April 4, 1893
Tomb Com.tee
J. Pierre
F. Vincent
M. Simons
R. Isaac
G. Jones

H. Lubin
G. Bacas
J. N. Cheri
Secty to Comm

A. J. Osey, Builder

Tomb 7: Tomb missing, MARCHAND

Tomb 8: (THNOC 66) BROLLE

Tomb 9: Tomb missing, PERAULT

Tomb 10: (THNOC 67) GARNIER (alternate apelling Garner); Boree; Henry (Louis, Sr., Sedonia Andry Desilva) (alternate spelling Destiva); Robertson

Garnier

In God we rest
Lillie Johnson Garnier
1885 – 1929

Alphonse Garnier, Jr.

1883 – 1939

Gilbert Garnier
1928 – 1946

Jeannette Garnier Garrett
1905 – 1960

Alphonsine Garnier Lewis
1903 – 1966

In memory of our dear mother
Sedonia Andry Desilva Henry
Born June 19 1908; died March 26, 1970

Louis Henry Sr.
Born March 4, 1908; died August 31, 1971

Tomb 11: (THNOC 68) DELACROIX; Blandin; Dinet (Antoinette)

Ici Repose
Francoise Orleux
Epouse de
Pierre Dinet
Nee a Pestelle, Ile St Dominique
Decede le 26 Juillet 1811
A l'age de 71 ans

Ici Repose
Antoinette Dinet
Nee a S. Yago Ile de Cuba
Decedee le 11 Decembre 1844
A l'age de 35 ans
Elle etait bonne soeur tender amie
Trep bonne pour la terre
Elle velait vers le cieux
(She was a good sister and a kind friend
From the earth she (went?) to the heavens)

Note: As of 2014, there's a board propped between Tomb 11 and Tomb 12. A new plaque with this same information is currently attached at Row F, Tomb 19 (THNOC 222).

Ici Repose
Marie Benjamin Dale
Epouse de Teophile Hazeur
Denoier (sic) le 15 De(c) 1844

Tomb 12: (THNOC 69) COURCELLE (alternate spelling Clarcelle, Colrcelle) (Marie Ophelia); Oliver (alternate spelling Olivier)

Ici repose
Marie Ophelia Courcelle
Nee le 26 Avril 1816
Decedee le 29 Septembre 1842

Tomb 13: (THNOC 70) Famille MA Garcia; GUESNON (alternate spelling Guenon) (Ursen; alternate spelling Ursin, Urson)

Famille M. A. Garcia

Ursin Guesnon
Decedee 29 Aout 18 __

Tomb 14: Tomb is missing, DUPLESSIS

Tomb 15: (THNOC 71) DEMZAELIERE (alternate spelling Demaeliere); Fazande (alternate spelling Fazende)

Demazeliere, Dessalles, Legaux

Adolph Demazeliere
March 17, 1886 – June 15, 1963, age 77 years

Lelia Dessalles
1890 – 1974

Charles J. Legaux
January 18, 1946 – September 30, 1985

216

Leticia Perez
Died February 29, 1923

Tomb 16: (THNOC 72) DUBRUEIL (alternate spelling Dubreuil, Dubrueil, Dubreuille)

Tomb 17: (THNOC 73) SOCIETY OF ST. HELEN (alternate spelling Society of St. Hellen); Viosin

Sainte Helen Societe de Bienfaisance Mutuelle

Signed: Callico (stonecutter)

Tomb 18: (THNOC 74) SOCIETY DE LOUISIANE

Tomb 19: (THNOC 75) TENOIR (alternate spelling Ternoir, Ternooir on the map)

Ternoir

A la memoire de
Jean Ternoir pere

Et de son epouse
Louise Millon

A dear mother
Mary Oliver

Died July 23, 1960

Tomb 20: (THNOC 76) SOCIETY DAMES ET DU SILENCE

Societe Dames et Demoiselle Du Silence
Fondee le 10 Novembre 1864
Incorporee le 17 Decembre 1888

Officers
Jos. Johnson Pres.
Eulalie Farr Vice Pres.
O. D. Pavageau Sec.
H. Amand Fin Sec
C. Labat Asst Sec
Louis Adams Treas

Tomb 21: (THNOC 77) SOCIETE DES DAMES DE ST. ANDRIE

Societe des Dames de St. Andre
Fondee le 15 Fevrier 1875

Tomb 22: (THNOC 78) POUPET (alternate spelling Pupet); ST CLOUD

Behind Tomb 22 (THNOC 78), between it and Row J, Tomb 22 (THNOC 91)

Note: This is part of a stone from Row K, Tomb 23 (THNOC 125), showing the names of William St. Leger, Lise Dodin, and D. Francois Rennaud.

Tomb 23: (THNOC 79) POREE

Famille Charles Poree

Edgar Poree
Died February 18, 1923, aged 57

Florville (marble-cutter)

Tomb 24: Tomb is missing; CABAREE

(Photo includes missing Tombs 24 – 25).

Tomb 25: Tomb is missing, SOCIETY OF ST. PIERRE

Tomb 26: (THNOC 80) GLAPION

Tablet on side:
Ci git
Rosalie Manent
Morte le 11 Juin 1843

Beloved Wife and Mother
Josephine Grubbs Glapion

November 29, 1911 – January 21, 1991

Our Loving Daddy and Friend
Walter A. Glapion, Sr.
June 25, 1910 – November 4, 1993

Fern Glapion Brady
August 9, 1931 – November 10, 1995

Tomb 27: (THNOC 81) SOCIETY of Ami Sol de L'Esperance

Societee des Amis de L'Esperance
Fondee Lee – Juin 1887
Incorporee le 30 Decembre 1867

Tomb 28: (THNOC 82) SISTERS OF CHRISTIAN CHARITY

Sisters of Christian Charity B.M.A.A.

Herman Ralph Deterville
Sgt US Army
World War II
1920 – 1976

2011
December 23

Note: Herman Deterville's wife, Althea, died December 17, 2011, so this notation may mark her burial.

Tomb 29: Tomb is missing; LACLOTTE (alternate spelling Laciotte)

Tomb 30: (THNOC 83) FOSTER

G. Foster

Tomb 31: (THNOC 84) BERNOUDY

A la memoire de
Mathilde Bernoudy
Epouse de Julien Colvis
Decedee le 6 Juin 1842
A l'age de 33 ans

Marie-Mathilde
Leur fille
Decedee a l'age 20 mois

Emma M.rie Bernoudy
Decedee le 11 Mars 1849

Marguerite Lacoste
Decedee le 13 Dec 1853
A l'age de 83 ans

Tomb signed lower front right "Monsseaus New Orleans"

Discrepancies:

Tomb 1 (THNOC 63) is listed as Tomb 36 on the SOC map, identified as Row NR. Next to it is a large plot, spanning Row I and Row J, which is listed as Tomb 35 on the SOC map. We are counting this same plot in both rows, since it takes the space of a tomb in both. Then our Tomb 3 (THNOC 64) is counted on the SOC map as Tomb 1. This puts our numbering two ahead of the SOC map numbering.

Tomb 13 (THNOC 70): The SOC spreadsheet puts the Famille M. A. Garcia in this tomb. The THNOC information shows "Famille M. A. Garcia" in Row K, Tomb 5 (THNOC 110). That tomb is visibly labeled "Famille M. A. Garcia." It is possible that there are two Famille M. A. Garcias. At least the name "Ursin Guenon" is clearly on Tomb 13 (THNOC 70).

ROW J
St. Peter's Aisle (Alley No. 2 -R), Left

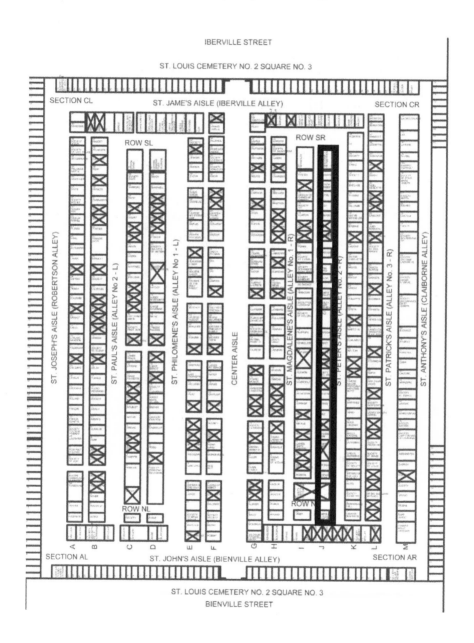

Row J: St. Peter's Aisle (Alley No. 2 - R)
Left Side

THNOC numbers 85 – 105

The tombs are counted as we're walking away from Bienville and toward Iberville, with Robertson to our left and Claiborne to our right.

Tomb 1: (THNOC 105) SOCIETE DE ST. LOUIS CONZCUR; Ganier (Jeanne R., Joseph L.); Laurent (Earnest J.); Sarazin (Augustine)

Societe de St Louis de Gonzague
Fondee le 1er Janvier 1854

Ernest J. Laurent
1893 – 1948

Augustine Sarazin
1877 – 1962

Jeanne R. Ganier
June 26, 1900 – July 20, 1969

Joseph L Ganier
Louisiana
Pvt Btry F351 FA92 DIV
World War I
October 19, 1893 – August 7, 1961
228

Tomb 2: Tomb is missing, SOCIETY OF CHRISTIAN DOCTRINE #1. The plot is big enough that it covers both Row I and Row J. See the photo for Row I, Tomb 2.

Tomb 3: (THNOC 104) POEYFAIR (alternate spelling Poeyfaire, Polyfarre) (Marie, Vincent, Joseph); VINCENT; Joly (Regine)

Joseph Vincent
Decedee le 6 Sept 1854
Age d'un ans

Regina Joly
Nee de Pauline Bertrand
Decedee le 3 Avril 1893
Agee de 21 ans

Ci-git
Marianne Polyfarre
Decedee 9 Avril 1811
Agee de 50 ans

Tomb 4: (THNOC 103) MONTREUL (Mattreul)

Tomb 5: Tomb is missing, SOCIETY des Demoiselles Sencere

Tomb 6: (THNOC 102) JOURDAN; PIRON (Albert L. Sr, Alice, Mary, Robert H.)

Say a Little Prayer

Piron

Albert Piron
Born February 25, 1925 – Died December 7, 1930

Alice Piron
Born December 31, 1891 – Died March 25, 1955

Mary Piron
Born July 23, 1930 – Died March 16, 1971

Aryand J. Piron, Jr.
Died May 9, 1937, age 24 years

Ici Repose
Francois Bierra
Ne le 4 Octobre 1811
Decedee le 20 Avril 1847

Louis Joseph Bierra

Henriette Elisabeth Beauvois
Epouse de Celestin Jourdan
Decedee le 18 Dec 1865
Agee de 79 ans

Marie Francoise Jourdan
Epouse de Francois Bie ___
Decedee le 18 Juille 1867
Agee de 55 ans

Adele Jourdan
Epouse de Milford Piron
Decedee le 14 May 1872

On back of tomb:

Tomb 7: Tomb is missing, JASON (alternate spelling Jasson)

Tomb 8: (THNOC 101) Society de Dames de Er; LOPEZ (Donald V., Sr., Hubert B., Josephine L.); Clark (Margaret L.); Graves (Charles E.); Jones (Albertine)

Societe Dames D'Esperance
Fondee le 23 Sept 1877

Margaret L. Clark
October 8, 1939 – May 27, 1999

Albertine "Bot" Jones
May 11, 1898 – January 29, 1986
Charles E. Graves
January 13, 1948 – October 27, 1998

Josephine Levy Lopez
"Josie"
September 9, 1911 – March 22, 2003

Donald V. Lopez, Sr.
March 23, 1936 – May 21, 2008

James A. Firmin
October 16, 1935 – November 2, 2004

Hubert Bernard Lopez
Sgt US Air Force
Korea Vietnam

January 20, 1934 – November 23, 1989

Tomb 9: (THNOC 100) LARRIEU (August, Clifford A. Jr, Jeanne F., John H.); Arnolia (Martha)

Famille Larrieu

Jeanne Fortier Larrieu
1885 – 1959

John M. Larrieu
1886 – 960
Martha Arnolia
1897 – 1980

Clifford A. Larrieu, Jr.
1942 – 1996

August Larrieu
1907 - 1982

Tomb 10: (THNOC 99) DUCLOLANGE (alternate spelling Duclolnge, Duclolang, Dulolanelle)

Ici repose
Edouard J. Duclolange
Decedee le 17 Juillet 1845
A l'age de 33 ans
Il fut bon pere et tender epoux.
(He was a good father and loving spouse)

Florville

Ici repose
Adolphe Plicque
Mort le 15 Mai 1895
Age de 79 ans

Ici repose
Zenon Victor
Ne a le N.velle Orleans
Morte le 16 Nov 1835
Age de 18 ans

Charlotte Victor
Epouse de H. Poree
Nee le 14 Fev 1811
Decedee le 24 Juillet 1840

Monsseaux and Trinchard (stonecutters)

Tomb 11: Tomb is missing, BLA: Montfort

Tomb 12: (THNOC 98) SOCIETY DE ST. VINCENT DE PAUL

Tomb 13: Tomb is missing; VANBOIGT

(Photo includes missing Tombs 13 – 14).

Tomb 14: Tomb is missing, CARRAICO

Tomb 15: (THNOC 97) AUBERT (B. Elizabeth, Louis V.)

Ci Git
V.ve Louis Aubert
Nee a l'Ile St. Dominque
Decedee le 24 Sept 1845
Agee de 92 ans
Et sa fille

B. Elizabeth Aubert
Decedee le 20 Dec 1866
A l'age de 74 ans

Tomb 16: (THNOC 96) CHARBONNET (Alcerdes); Fleitas (J. Frankline)

In memory of our dear daughter
Alcerdes Charbonnet
Born June 25, 1932; died February 23, 1955, age 22 years

Ici repose
J. Frankline Fleita
Decedee le 28 Novembre 184(1)
Agee de 27 ans

Tomb 17: LOPEZ (No THNOC number). This was a missing tomb at the time of the THNOC survey, which has since been restored.

Tomb 18: (THNOC 95) SOCIETY AMOUR ETERNELLE (alternate spelling Society of Eternelle Lamcor)

Pediment: **Les Enfant Amoure (--)ern Su (--)**
Organized September 11, 1871
Building Committee:
Rita Sylvan, M. Love, F. Chaligny, O. Fortune, Builder

Officers
Rita Sylvan, Mother
M. Love, Pres
L. Poree, Vic Pres

M. Foree, Chr. Relief Com.
J. Edwards, Sec
M. Willis, Tres.

Tomb 19: (THNOC 94) SOCIETY OF MORALITY (alternate spelling
Society of Moraliti)

Tomb 20: (THNOC 93) TAYLOR (Felicie); Bousiere; Coker (Louise);
Henriques

Taylor

In memory of our

Dear Mother
Felicie Taylor
Died November 29, 1954

Louise T. Coker
Died February 2, 1976

Tomb 21: (THNOC 92) GODIN; HAINS (alternate spelling Haines)
(Manuel Sr.)

Family Manuel Hains, Sr

Between Tomb 21 (THNOC 92) and Tomb 22 (THNOC 91), there is a
new stone on the ground.

Roscoe J. Boguille, Sr.
January 26, 1918 – November 14, 1986

Marion J. Boguille
July 29, 1914 – November 19, 1990

Roscoe J. Boguille, Jr.
September 13, 1939 – June 8, 1994

Tomb 22: (THNOC 91) MONROSE (Joseph); Castele (Paul)

Ici repose

Marcelin I. Monrose
Ne a la N. Orleans
Decedee le 10 Decembre 1877
A l'age de 19 ans

Josephine Monrose
Decedee 25 Decembre 1851
A l'age de 3 mois 15 jours

Augustine Monrose
Decedee le 13 Decembre 1851
A l'age de 4 ans 4 mois

Cit git
Joseph Monrose
Ne a Miragouane, Ile S. D. (Santo Domingo)

Decedee 4 Novembre 1832
A l'age de 45 ans

Paul Castele
Louisiana
MA JC USNRF
World War I
November 26, 1893
July 25, 1947

Tomb 23: Tomb is missing, LABOULET (alternate spelling Labouoier)

(Photo includes missing Tombs 23 – 24).

Tomb 24: Tomb is missing. No names.

Tomb 25: (THNOC 90) LABEAUD (Honore); Thomas

Ci-git
Rosette Rousseve
Decedee le 18 Sept 1832
Agee de 76 ans

Ici repose
Honore Labeaud
Decedee le 21 Janvier 1836
Age de 48 ans

Isnard (stonecutter)

Tomb 26: (THNOC 89) Remy; BELOT (V.)

V. Beloit

Jeanne

Thomas R (--)y

Tomb 27: (THNOC 88) BOUTTE; Dupuis (alternate spelling Dupui) (Luiele); Fastio (M. Claire)

Louise (---)

(some illegible lines)

Aupres (d'elle) repose

(Beside her lies)

M Cla (--) Fastio

Decedee le 14 Avril 18(--)

A l'age de 77 ans

(--)ill Dupuis

Epouse de F. P. (Boulle)

Decedee le 6 Jan 184(9) a l'age de 36 ans

Tomb 28: (THNOC 87) CARRIDA, CORDIER

Famille F. Cordier

A ma Fille

Tomb 29: (THNOC 86) GAIGNARD (alternate spelling Goegoari) (Emelie Louise); Barthelmy (Clementine)

Ici repose
Emelie Louise Gaignard
Nee a la croire de bouequets
Ile St Domique
Le 4 Aout 179(5)
Morte le 27 Nov 1846
Note: The Saint-Domingue village Croix-de-Bouquets sank below sea level in a 1770 earthquake, and was later relocated.
Clementine Barthelmy
Morte le 30 Mars 1891
A l'age de 85 ans

Tomb 30: (THNOC 85) SOCIETY DES DAMES DE PROVIDENCE

Sous Le Patronage de Sainte Anne
La Providence Societe de Dames et DeMoisselles

Discrepancies:

Tomb 2: This is a large, empty plot, which spans Row I and Row J, and is listed as Tomb 35 on the SOC map. We are counting this same plot in both rows, since it takes the space of a tomb in both. Then our Tomb 3 (THNOC 104) is counted on the SOC map as Tomb 2. This puts our numbering one ahead of the SOC map numbering.

Tomb 17: The SOC map shows this as "16/17," possibly because the plot is very large. This tomb was crossed off at the time of the THNOC survey, and does not have a THNOC number, implying the plot was empty at the time. The handwritten SOC map also shows this plot unlabeled, but the updated SOC map and spreadsheet show the name Lopez. As of 2014, there is a large and obviously new tomb in the spot for Lopez.

Because the next tomb is Tomb 18 (THNOC 95), the numbering becomes consistent again after this point.

ROW K
St. Peter's Aisle (Alley No. 2 -R), Right

IBERVILLE STREET

ST. LOUIS CEMETERY NO. 2 SQUARE NO. 3

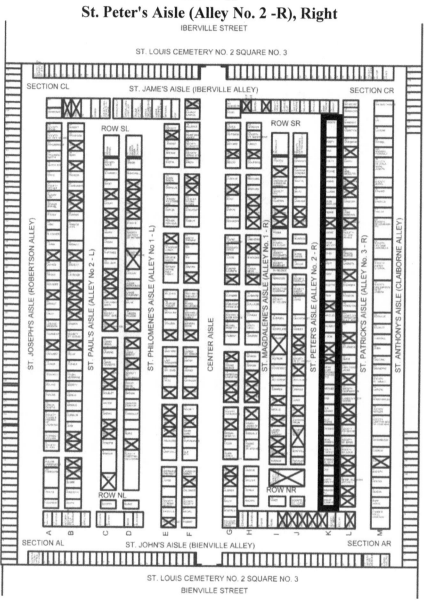

249

Row K: St. Peter's Aisle (Alley No. 2 - R
Right Side

THNOC numbers 106 – 137

The tombs are counted as we're walking away from Bienville and toward Iberville, with Robertson to our left and Claiborne to our right.

Tomb 1: (THNOC 106) LAMBERT; ROUSSEVE

Ici reposent
George Rousseve
Ne le 22 Fevrier 1835
Decedee le (7) Avril 1836

Jeanne Rousseve
Nee le 21 Juin 183(7)
Decedee le 20 Auot 1839
E(t)

Jean B. Rousseve
Ne le 2 Janvier 1821
Decedee le 26 Fevrier 18(4)1

Tomb 2: (THNOC 107) PERRARNAUD (alternate spelling Perarnaud); HALL

Ici repose
(Henri) (P)
(les laisse)
(leaves)
A l'age de (21) ans

Tomb 3: (THNOC 108) SOCIETY OF SACRE COEUR

As of 2016, there was a planter in front with an inscription:

Happy Father's Day 2016 to My Rock
My Daddy

Melvin Anthony Johnson, Sr.

Tomb 4: (THNOC 109) REISS (Regina); Cheverre (alternate spelling Chevrelle)

Regina Reiss
Wife of Henry Martin
Died June 3, 1926, age 42 years

Tomb 5: (THNOC 110) SISTERS OF THE HOLY FAMILY; M.H. Garcia

Famille M. A. Garcia

Sisters of the Holy Family

Tomb 6: (THNOC 111) SOCIETY DE VIOLETTE

Ladies of Violes B. M. A. A.
Organized March 2, 1884
Incorporated April 12, 1886

Tomb 7: (THNOC 112) CHEVAL; HERRIMAN; Brown (Anthony); Leon (Francois, Henry, Thomas, Victoria); Papin (Victoria); Trevigne (Paul)

Ici Repose

Sylvanie Catherine Brunetti
Epouse de Francois Leon
Nee a la Nouvelle Orleans le Mai 1881
Decedee le 24 Aout 18

Note: The name Paul Trevigne is noted here in the SOC spreadsheet. Paul Trevigne (1825 – 1908) was the editor and a writer of the newspaper *L'Union*, cited as the first African-American newspaper, which operated from 1962 – 1864. I have been unable to verify any information about Trevigne's burial, to determine if this is the same person.

Tomb 8: (THNOC 113) HERRIMAN; Cheval (alternate spelling Cherval)

Cheval

Herriman

Famille F. Herriman

Tomb 9: (THNOC 114) BAILLY (Mad Narcisse); CATORIE (alternate spelling Catoire, Catore)

Ci-Git
Madame Narcisse Bailly
Nee le 19 Janvier 1832
Decedee le 6 Avril 1845

El, avec se mere
Annette Catoire
Epouse de N. Bailly
Morte le 22 Sept 1856
A l'age de 60 ans, 4 mois, 22 jours

Septima

Tomb 10: (THNOC 115) ROUX (alternate spelling Rouxi) (Marie Adele); CARRABY; Carraico (B. George); Loustalet

( ) de
Victoire (Broul)
V.ve Artig ( )
( ) le 2( ) Aout 18(11)
(A l'age de 18 ans)
(--) Dec 1902

George B Carraby
Louisiana
Sgt Army Air Forces
World War II
February 3, 1915 – May 25, 1967

Tomb 11: (THNOC 116) VIARD (alternate spelling Viaud); Bergeron (W. Edna); Curlel (Marie): Espy (E. Russell, James, John Russell, Alma Morand); Morand (Delmar, Favelin Louise); Palao (J. Edward); Pittman (McKinley); Quevain (alternate spelling Quelain) (Louise Clare);Ward (Louise M.)

James Espy
Pvt US Army
World War I
September 11, 1890 – August 25, 1977

Edward J. Palao
Born November 18, 1886; died November 30, 1964

Delmar Morand
Born February 15, 1874; died April 15, 1970

Russell John Espy
Born November 28, 1953; died May 7, 1965
At Wills Point, LA

Alma Morans Espy
July 12, 1911 – September 20, 1988

Russell E. Espy
May 29, 1902 – April 20, 1995

Louise Favelin Morand
Born August 24, 1878; died June 2, 1943

Ici reposent
M. Louise Viard
Morte le 17 Mars 1837
A l'age de 60 ans

Claire Louise Quevain
Epouse de J. Curiel
Morte le 21 Aout 1849

Edna W. Bergeron
January 2, 1919, age 24 yrs.

Marie Curiel
July 11, 1938, age 83 yrs.

Tomb 12: (THNOC 117) MARTINEZ (C. Jeane, J. Ferdinand Sr.);
Boisdore; Schultz (S. Jose)

Jos E Schulze
Died January 24, 1938

Tomb 13: (THNOC 118) OWENS (Arthur, Donta Rose, J. Arthur, S.
Rose); MILLER (B. Angelina, Earl, Stephen); PRATCHER (Pete Henry);
HARCISSE (alternate spelling Narcisse) (Frank); BOYD (Dorita Owens);
Astie

Dorita Rose Owens

Arthur Owens
June 17, 1881 – November 18, 1930

Stephen Miller
September 15, 1885 – June 16, 1937

Henry Pete Pratcher
December 1, 1919 – July 20, 1949

Earl Miller
December 30, 1913 – April 21, 1962

Angelina B. Miller
August 18, 1889 – April 11, 1964

Rose S. Owens
February 12, 1893 – November 6, 1966

Frank Narcisse
August 5, 1915 – December 5, 1980

Arthur J. Owens
August 27, 1928 – August 4, 1982

Dorita Owens Boyd
April 2, 1926 – March 22, 1990

Tomb 14: Tomb is missing.

(Photo includes missing Tombs 14 – 15).

Tomb 15: Tomb is missing. Barbet; Burnette (Nelson Eunice); Nelson (Heaton Clothilde, Morris)

Tomb 16: (THNOC 119) NELSON; Pena; Percy

Morris Nelson
Louisiana
OS US Navy
June 10, 1881 – April 24, 1957
In loving memory of
Eunice Nelson Burnette

Died October 31, 1947

Clothilde Heaton Nelson
Died January 7, 1971

Tomb 17: (THNOC 120) CHAUMBETTE (alternate spelling Chaumbet, Chaumette)

Note: At the time of the Tablet Survey, an illegible tablet was noted, leaning against the tomb. That tablet was gone by 2016.

Tomb 18: (THNOC 121) MARCELIN (alternate spelling Marccelis); Monthieu (Montegut)

Marcelin Famille

Tomb 19: Missing tomb, CRAWFORD

Tomb 20: (THNOC 122) TESON

Jules M. Roussel
Died March 3, 1945

Ici repose
(Bos) – Gu. Rit
Decedee ()9 Juin 1816
A l'age de (--) ans.

Tomb 21: (THNOC 123) COLLETTE (alternate spelling Colette, Cobette)

Ici reposent
M. Louise C. Olette
Veuve Nicolas Maran
Decedee le 16 Nov 1839
Agee den viron 90 ans

V.ve Arthur Valentin
Nee le 10 Juin 1776
Morte le 7 Fev 1863
Bonne mere regrette par sa famille
(A good mother regretted by her family)

Tomb 22: (THNOC 124) GROSS; Philip (Clarence Lionel); Phoenix
(Joseph); Williams (Manuel)

There are three smaller headstones in front of the tomb.

Manuel I. Williams
Pvt US Army
World War II
November 26, 1906 – July 12, 1988

Lionel Clarence Philip
AMM3 US Navy
World War II
August 26, 1926 – November 4, 1996

Joseph Phoenix
Pvt US Army
March 18, 1924 – March 3, 1993

Tomb 23: (THNOC 125) KNIGHT (D. Eugenia, Luke); Society St. K. DePaul

Renaud

Joseph Renaud
Ne le 1.er Sept 1847
Morte dans le meme annee
Regretted de sa l'annette
(Died in the same year,
Regretted by his Annette)

Ici reposent
Constan Michel
Ne a Port au Prince Ile S.D.
En 1780
Decede 14 Aout 18 ..

Sa fille
Uranie
Decedee le 4 Avril 1845,
A l'age de 31 ans

Eulalie Michel
Decedee le 24 Juin 1848
A l'age de 27 ans

William St. Leger

Decede le 15 Nov 1852
A l'age de 49 ans

Lise Dodin
Decedee le 10 Sept 1858
A l'age de 85 ans

D. Francois Rennaud
Nee Clara Michel
Decedee le 21 Aout 1860
A l'age de (4) ans

Eugenia D. Knight
1904 – 1981

Luke Knight
1899 - 1984

Nelder (marble-cutter)

Note: Part of a tablet from this tomb is now set in the ground behind Row I, Tomb 22.

Tomb 24: (THNOC 126) MICHEL (alternate spelling Michael) (Constance)

Ci-git
M.lle Constance Michel
Nee a le Jamaique le 30 Dec 1801
Decedee le 10 Mars 1835

Tomb 25: (THNOC 127) VICTOR; CUIELLETTE (alternate spelling Collette) (Anathalie, E. George, E. Palmyra); Barre (Lawrence); Lavigne; Samuel (Marguerite Blanc); Slie (Stanley, Theresa)

Famille Cuiellette

George E. Cuiellette
1892 – 1955

Edgar Cuiellette
1891 – 1903

Anathalie Cuiellette
Age 73

Marguerite Samuel
Age 65

Stanley Slie
1907 – 1936

Palmyra E. Cuiellette
1901 – 1936

Theresa Slie
Died February 4, 1937

Lawrence Barre, Jr
1920 – 1937

Tomb 26: **(THNOC 128)** LAVIGNE

Celeste Ladner
Nee le 21 Avril 1793
Morte le 9 Juin 1855

Leon et Virginie Lavigne
Morte en bas age
(Died at a young age)

(Florville)

Tomb 27: Missing tomb.

Tomb 28: (THNOC 129) ETIENNE; Snaer

Ferdinand Etienne
Decedee le 10 Dec 1873
A l'age de 63 ans

D.me Vidalise Elisabeth Duplessis
V.ve de Ferdinand Etienne
Decedee le 11 Mars 1880
A l'age de 69 ans

Tomb 29: (THNOC 130) LES DEMOISELLES Sinceres; Daste; Duplessis
(Vidalise Elisabeth); Dusuah; Elienne (Ferdinand)

Les Demoiselles Sinceres
Societe de Bienfaisance Mutuelle
Sous le Patronage de La Tres Ste. Vierge
(Under the patronage of the Most Holy Virgin)
Fondet le 15 Oct 1871
Dimisee le 30 Oct 1877
Reorganized le 1st Nov 1877
Et incorpore e 2 Nov 1877

F. J. Duplessis Fondateur (marble-cutter)

Tomb 30: **(THNOC 131)** WILLIAMS

(Ici) Repose

( ) me Snaer
Morte le 2 Mai 1838
Agee de 28 ans
La vertu guidait ses actions
(Virtue guided his actions)

WILLIAMS

Herbert Johnson
January 1, 1895 – March 31, 1964

Beulah Johnson
December 15, 1894 – April 6, 1976

Tomb 31: (THNOC 132) THOMAS; Desvignes; Johnson (Bevian, Herbert); Williams

Tomb 32: (THNOC 133) BATCAVE; Thomas

Ici reposent
Marie Jeanne Batcave
Nee a St. Marc, Ile St. Dominique
Morte le 18 Juille 1842 a l'age de 87 ans

Son fils
P. Zami Batcave
Ne a l'ile St. Dominique
Decedee le 29 Oct 1843, a l'age de 44 ans

Eunice Mary St. Amand
Born December 8, 1913; died October 28, 1918

Tomb 33: (THNOC 134) SOCIETY of St. Alphonse

Societe de Bien.ce et l Ass.ce Mu.elle
La P.tion de St. Alp.se de Ligoury,
Le 5 Sep 1860

Tomb 34: (THNOC 135) CRAIG

Note: At the time of the Tablet Survey, there was a leaning, broken tablet behind this tomb, but it was gone as of 2016:

Famille Perreault and Bazanac

Alcee

Tomb 35: (THNOC 136) SOCIETY de St. Laurent; Roberts

In Memory
Adele Eugene
December 3, 1941

John Herere, Sr.
September 24, 1954

Xenophan Luster
March 27, 1940 – November 11, 1971

Jeanne Herere
September 21, 1880 – February 9, 1978

Edward Montana
July 29, 1921 – December 31, 1995

Marcelle Montana
August 26, 1921 – June 3, 1998

Bruce Luster
September 27, 1955 – June 20, 2014

Alice Montana

May 22, 1900 – January 11, 2000

Allison Montana
December 16, 1922 – June 27, 2005

Madeline Luster
July 22, 1920 – March 17, 2014

Tomb 36: **(THNOC 137)** ROBERTS (Evgenia D. Bazile); Dominguez (alternate name Dominkueuz ,Domingue); Lambert; Leaumont; Roberts (Bobbie R.L. Sr.) (alternate spelling Robertson)

Roberts

Eugenia D. Bazile
May 23, 1890 – June 2, 1982

Margaret Bazile Roberts
April 1, 1926 – January 28, 2016

Bobbie R. L. Roberts, Sr.
May 28, 1925 – July 17, 1989

Gregory A. R. Roberts
August 10, 1958 – July 6, 2011

Lillian Dominguez
April 15, 1898 – January 30, 1939

Joseph A Labeaud
Louisiana
Pvt US Army
World War I
September 9, 1896 – August 5 1958

Discrepancies
Row K: St. Peter's Aisle

Tomb 7 (THNOC 112): The updated SOC spreadsheet and map show this is "Cheval, Herriman," and Tomb 8 (THNOC 113) as "Herriman, Cheval." The handwritten SOC map shows Tomb 7 as "Leon" and Tomb 8 as "Herriman." Tomb 8 (THNOC 113) has "Cheval Herriman" visibly carved on it, so we have to assume that the handwritten map was correct, and "Leon" is in Tomb 7.

Tomb 15: the SOC spreadsheet puts Eunice Nelson Burnette and Clothilde Heaton Nelson in this missing tomb, and "Nelson" in Tomb 16 (THNOC 119). These two names are clearly visible on Tomb 16 (THNOC 119), so that is correct.

Tomb 22: On the handwritten SOC map, this is listed as Society of St. V. De Paul. The updated spreadsheet shows the name Gross.

Tomb 23 (THNOC 125): This is labeled on the SOC map as Tomb 22A. The next tomb (our Tomb 24) is numbered on their map as Tomb 23. This makes our numbers one ahead of the SOC numbering until Tomb 35 (THNOC 137).

Tombs 23 and 24 are both labeled "Michel" on the handwritten SOC map, and the THNOC info shows Michels in both tombs. In Tomb 23 (THNOC 125), the THNOC information shows some Renauds, and one" D. Francois Rennaud, nee Clara Michel," so they could well be two family tombs next door to one another. The updated SOC map shows "Knight" at our Tomb 23.

Tomb 36 (THNOC 137): The SOC map, which has been one behind our numbering since our Tomb 23 (which they counted as Tomb 22A), catches up here at the end of the row. They count the large plot at Tomb 36 as "35/36."

ROW L
St. Patrick's Aisle (Alley No. 3 - R), Left

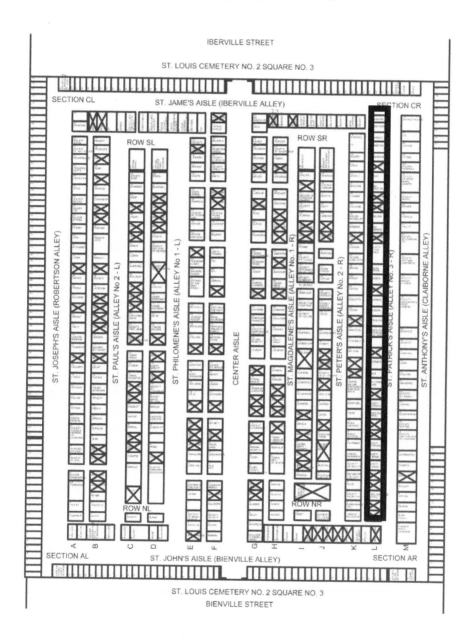

Row L: St. Patrick's Aisle (Alley No. 3 - R) Left Side

THNOC numbers 138 – 164

The tombs are counted as we're walking away from Bienville and toward Iberville, with Robertson to our left and Claiborne to our right.

Tomb 1: (THNOC 164) Missing tomb. This was still standing at the time of the THNOC Survey, listed as "No name, no tablet."

(Photo includes missing Tombs 1 – 2).

The map in the NAACP pamphlet shows Eugene Rapp in Row L, Tomb 1. The SOC map shows Eugene Rapp in St. Patrick's Aisle M, Tomb 2, which is just opposite, across the aisle.

Tomb 2: (THNOC 163) Missing tomb. This was still standing at the time of the THNOC Survey: "No inscriptions … now crumbling brick." There is nothing on SOC map for this tomb, but the SOC spreadsheet = Society of DeMarie H*

Tomb 3: (THNOC 162) DEDE; BARBARIN (Josephine Arshidere) (alternate spelling Arthidore); Dede (Louis); MITCHELL (Peter T.); Petit

Josephine Arthidore Barbarin
1876 – 1931

Ci git
Louis Dede
Decedee le 15 Juin 18(31)
Age de 65 ans

Peter T. Mitchell
Louisiana, STM 2 US Navy
World War II
April 4, 1921 – July 10, 1971

Tomb 4: Missing tomb, nothing on SOC map. SOC spreadsheet = Cazelar

(Photo includes missing Tombs 4 – 5).

Tomb 5: Missing tomb, nothing on SOC map. SOC spreadsheet = Galle

Tomb 6: (THNOC 161) SOCIETY of ST. LOUIS

Les Souers de St. Louis
Sous la protection de Jesus
Fondee le 1st Mai 185(1)

Tomb 7: (THNOC 160) SOCIETY ST. BIRBE (alternate spelling Society of St. Barbe)

Societe de Ste. Barbe de Bienfaisance Mutelle
Sous la protection de la Ste. Vierge
Fondee le 9 Janvier 1892
Incorporee le 5 Mai 1881

Tomb 8: (THNOC 159) SOCIETY of PROSPERITE

:
Hart-Croen Family

Tomb 9: Missing tomb; nothing on SOC map. SOC spreadsheet = Babet

(Photo includes missing Tombs 9 – 10).

Tomb 10: Missing tomb; nothing on SOC map

Tomb 11: (THNOC 158) LADIES SOCIETY of HARRIS

**Ladies of Veterans of
1862 & 1865, No. 1**

Founders
Mrs. (M) Lewis & Mr. James Lewis

Note: According to the NAACP pamphlet, founder James Lewis served
in the Union Army, later becoming a prominent member of the state
militia, and a Metropolitan Police officer, while remaining involved in
politics.

Tomb 12: (THNOC 157) SOCIETY of COOPERATIVE

Co-Operators Fraternells B.M.A.A.
Organized May 10, 1884
Incorporated February, ( ) 1887

L. B. Vignes
E. Lavigne
Jas. Remy, Builder
1216 Prytania St.

L. Porche Pres
L. H. Mathieu Chairm.
L. B. Vignes
Ed Populus
J. O. Cusman
G. V. Watts
A. E. Saloy
J. Styles
Geo. Doyle
W. Washington

Tomb 13: Missing tomb; Dawson

Tomb 14: (THNOC 156) DUPLESSIS; JACKS; Roudanez (Rose)

Famille of Duplessis and Jacks

Ito E. Jacks
December 1932

Tomb 15: (THNOC 155) SMITH; Ladies of Veterans; Lewis (James, M.)

Emelie Smith
Epouse de OC Blandin
Nee le 11 Nov 1843
Dec le 10 Mar 1880.

Callico (marble-cutter)

Note: By 2014, the tomb was buckling.

Tomb 16: (THNOC 154) FOURNIER (alternate spelling Fourniew);
Lamaison; Morel

Fournier

Tomb 17: Missing tomb; Manega

(Photo includes missing Tombs 17 – 18).

Tomb 18: Missing tomb, nothing on SOC map

Tomb 19: (THNOC 153) LADIES COOPERATION M.A.E. ASSOC; Barche (L.); Doyle (Geo.); Gusman (J. O.); Lavigne (E.); Matthew (L.H.); Remy (Jos.); Saloy (A. E.); Styles (J.); Vignes (L. B.); Washington (W.); Watts (G. V.)

Ladies Co-Operators M.A.B. Association
Organized September 4, 1892

Incorporated January 24, 1893

"Jungel"

E. A. Bigard, Builder

Committee
Mrs. S. Gregroire
Miss E. Severe
Miss A. Gasquet
Mr. G. V. Watts
Mr. A. E. Saloy
Miss A. Angelin
Ex officio, 1895

Tomb 20: (THNOC 152) HENDERSON; DeJean (alternate spelling Dejan) (Marie); Francis (Cecile, Nerbert)

Famille Henderson

Francoise Dutuet
Nee a Jeremie de D'Haiti
Mort en de 15 ans

Mrs. Marie Dejean

Norbert Francis

Cecile D. Francis
March 11, 1901 – September 16, 1976

Tomb 21: (THNOC 151) POINSON; Bertrand

Edvige Anna Poinson
July 29, 1919 – February 13, 2008

Lulma Lafaye

Tomb 22: (THNOC 150) BACHMAN; Wilson

Ici Repose
Charles Pierre
Ne le 1 Sept 1797

Decedee le le. Nov 1834 (sic)

Il fesait le Bonheur de sa famille
(He was the happiness of the family)

In loving memory of
Mary Bachemin
May 1, 1857 – July 3 1940

In loving memory of
Fabio Bachemin
Born May 18, 1905
Died January 3, 1934

Vera Rillieux
Died Sept 17, 1963

Tomb 23: Missing tomb; Plest

Tomb 24: (THNOC 149) LACASTE

Gex

Lacost

MOTHER, HUSBAND

Tomb 25: (THNOC 148) DUBOIS (Ulysses J., Ulysses Joseph Jr.);
BURTHE (alternate spelling Burton); Roy (alternate spelling Ray)
(Constance)

Gustavie Roy
Born December 15, 1872; died January 26, 1931

Ulysses S. Dubois
Born January 24, 1870; died January 2, 1930

Tomb 26: (THNOC 147) SOCIETY ST. VERANIQUE (alternate spelling St. Verokique), Cupidon (alternate spelling Cupebon)

Tablet leaning against tomb:
Rosalie Molosain
Nee a St. Morelle S. D.
Decedee le 11 Juin 1889, agee de 90 ans

Gertude Cupidon
Native de St. Mare, Ile St. Dominique
Decedee le 26 Oct 1818, agee de 50 ans

Tomb 27: Missing tomb; Bertonneau; Cronwell

Tomb 28: (THNOC 146) JUNG (alternate spelling Juing); RONGPRE (alternate spelling Longpre)

Jos. Clizac
Decedee le 28 Fev. 1907, age de 73 ans

Tomb 29: (THNOC 145) CAILLOUX

At rest

Anton Porel

Anita Porel

Lucia ? (sic, from THNOC)

Lawrence ? (sic, from THNOC)

"At foot of tomb, letters P.I.A. are painted" (from THNOC).

Note: This is the only tomb I can find in St. Louis #2 associated with the name Cailloux. Andre Cailloux "lauded as the nation's first black military hero" (Ochs 1) died May 27, 1863. Accounts agree that he was buried with great fanfare in St. Louis #2, and Ochs places him "possibly" (and most plausibly) in Square 3.

Tomb 30: Missing tomb; Mercier

(Photo includes missing Tombs 30 – 31).

Tomb 31: Missing tomb; Beauchamp (Beauclair) (in original); Munier

Tomb 32: (THNOC 144) NOEL; DESLATTE

Tomb 33: (THNOC 143) BARTH

Louis Barthe
Louisiana
PFC COC 313 Svc BN QMC
World War I
May 10, 1894 – November 12, 1964

Louis F Banjamin
Died April 23, 1946

Babet Lartigue
Decedee le 28 Nov 1833
A l'age de 70 ans

Augustine Dauphin
Nee le 16 Fev 1801
Decedee le 18 Mai 1858

Ambroise Barthe
Ne le 5 Avril 1862 Decedee le 11 Dec 1862

M.me Irma Barthe
Nee le 27 Oct 1863 Decedee le 1.er Juin 1864

E(ne) Melicert Barthe
Nee le 15 Nov 1859 Decedee le 28 Juin 1864

Antoine D. Barthe
Decede le 23 Dec 1896 age de 16 ans

Antoine Barthe
Decedee le 27 Jan 1904 age de 77 ans

Irma Louise Delval
Epouse Antoine Barthe
Decedee le 19 Sept 1909 agee de 52 ans

Tomb 34: Missing tomb; Allgre

Tomb 35: (THNOC 142) CASANAVE (alternate spelling Cazenave; both appear on tomb)

Felix Desvignes
1886 – 1940

Ellen Casanave
1863 – 1953

Salome Desvignes
1889 – 1960

Ursul D. Reed
December 4, 1910 – March 19, 1981

Eloina D. Cazenave
July 16, 1912 – January 14, 1984

Edgar J. Reed
September 20, 1901 – November 18, 1992

Note: The NAACP pamphlet states that the Casanave Family was one of the wealthiest black families in the 19th century.

Tomb 36: (THNOC 141) LEBRETON

Lebreton

Paul Brown
March 7, 1924 – Still Born

Marie DePass
December 8, 1871 – November 25, 1952

Gertrude Lumas
November 12, 1899 – December 9, 1970

Alice Stanley
June 21, 1902 – December 16, 1970

Estelle Brown
March 31, 1997 – August 8, 1980

Tomb 37: (THNOC 140) MANEILLE (alternate spelling Manette);
Manneville (Jeanne) (Probably Manneville?)

Ici + Git
Jeanne Manneville
Nee a la __
Decedee la 13 Jan 1837
Age de 52 ans

Tomb 38: (THNOC 139) BRADFORD; Gaudin; Johnson

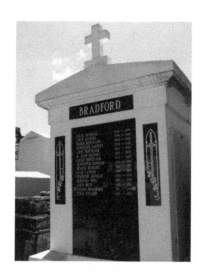

Famille H. C. Gaudin

Ce monument et consacre paient
Eopoux pieux et sensible,
A la memoire d'une bonne femme.
(This monument and sacred devotion is paid
By a pious and senstivie husband
To the memory of a good woman)

Aline Johnson
Morte le 18 Nov 1864
Agee de 39 ans

H. Gaudin
Morte le 18 Dec 1855
Age de 5 mois

Adele Neguitte
Morte le 22 Mars 1864
Agee de 12 ans

Carriere Gaudin
Mort le 5 Mai 1864
Age de 2 ans et 5 mois

Clarisse Gaudin
Morte le 15 Mai 1866
Agee de 10 ans

Bradford

Elise B. Lacroix
1866 – 1919

Sylvania L. Pero
1890 – 1950

Jules Janneau
1834 – 1899

Louis Lacroix
1899 – 1899

Marie Bertrand
1884 – 1900

Ernestine Lacroix
1886 – 1903

Louis Bertrand
1837 – 1907

A. Jean Jacques
1881 – 1908

Louise Bertrand
1847 – 1909

Genevieve Janneau
1841 – 1916

Helene Beaulieu
1866 – 1917

Alice Muse
1893 – 1950

Vivian Bradford
1911 – 1982

Lydia Villere
1913 – 1992

Callico (marble-cutter)

Tomb 39: (THNOC 138) BOISDORE

(No name)
Ne le 19 Aout 1890
Mort le 25 Aout 1926
A l'age de 36 ans

Discrepancies
Row L: St. Patrick's Aisle

Unusually, this row has a lot of tombs on the SOC map that were crossed off, and don't have any names on them.

Tomb 1 (THNOC 164): The SOC spreadsheet gives a list of names that seem to belong to Tomb 3 (THNOC 162). It's possible that they were relatives with a nearby tomb, which wouldn't be unprecedented, but it seems likely that they belong to Tomb 3.

Tomb 148 and 149 (spreadsheet vs. map)

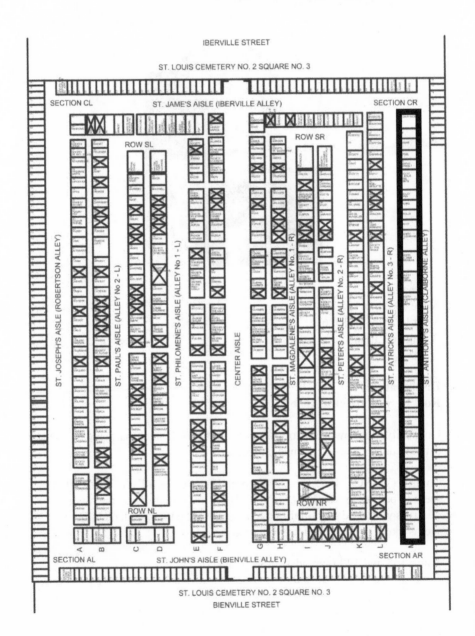

Row M: St. Patrick's Aisle (Alley No. 3 - R) Right Side

THNOC numbers 174 – 205

The tombs are counted as we're walking away from Bienville and toward Iberville, with Robertson to our left and Claiborne to our right.

Tomb 1: (THNOC 174) FOUNIER; ADELE; DAVIDSON (alternate spelling Daivdson); Baptiste; Davidson (George Sr.)

Adele

George Davidson Sr.
Born February 19, 1866; died June 27, 1938

Founier Family

Tomb 2: (THNOC 175) RAPP (Dame Eugene, Madame Eugene); DUBUC; Collins (Wilared E.)

Famille Eugene Rapp

Dame Eugene Rapp
Nee Alphonse Philomene Rey
Decedee le 14 Mars 1894

Wilfred E. Collins
Died September 2, 1912

M.me Eugene Rapp
Nee Aline Philomene Staes
Decedee le 27 Mai 1919

J. Karcher (marble-cutter)

Note: The NAACP pamphlet's map shows the tomb of Eugene Rapp
opposite this one, across the aisle at Row L, Tomb 1, but the name Eugene
Rapp is on this tomb, so it's the likely spot. According to the pamphlet,
Rapp was an officer in a black Confederate militia, who became Union
officers after the take-over of New Orleans by northern forces.

Tomb 3: (THNOC 176) DEJEAN (Freddie J., Sr.)

Freddie J. DeJean, Sr.
US Air Force
Korea
January 6, 1933 – December 22, 1970

Tomb 4: (THNOC 177) GOUGIS (alternate spelling Gouguet)
(Ferdinand); Caro (Mildred Saloy); Cousin (Leah); Saloy (Corinne Gougis,
Olga Fitch)

Famille Louis Gougis

Ferdinand C. Gougis

1886 – 1954

Corinne Gougis Saloy

Mildred Saloy Caro
1914 – 1978

Leah Cousin (THNOC transcribes as "Leak")
1900 – 1938

Olga Fitch Saloy
1907 - 1986

Tomb 5: (THNOC 178) SOCIETY of De La Branche

Tomb 6: Missing tomb; Silvestri (Silvestre)

Tomb 7: (THNOC 179) LACROIX (alternate spelling Cacroix, Acroix, Genela Hermo F); Barthe (Clifford); Estevez (Dame Antoine); Heloise; Joseph (Jean); Ripoli (Beardell Barthe)

(In) memory of my beloved husband
Clifford Barthe
(Bo)rn October 20, 1912 – Died July 22, 193( )

In memory of my beloved wife
( )eardell Barthe Ripoll( )
(Bo)rn June 30, 1931 – Died Mar 20, 194( )
+

A la memoire de
F. Hermogene Lacroix
Ne le 13 Avril 1834
Decede a l'age de 13 ans

Jean Joseph
Decede le 20 Mars 1849
A l'age de 23 ans
Il est regrette de sa famille.

Dame Antoine Esteves
Decedee le 19 Decembre 1894
A l'age de 57 ans

Tomb 8: (THNOC 180) WASHINGTON (Isidore)

Washington Family

Isidore Tuts
1907 - 1984

Tomb 9: (THNOC 181) SOCIETY of LADY FRIENDS OF LOUISIANA

Ladies Friends of Louisiana B.M.A.A.

Officers
Fannie E. Washington, President
Violet Jones Vice
Rosa Benjamin Rec. Secty
Corinne R. Azamere Fin
Organized October 14, 1900
:
Building committee
Thomas Torregano Chairman
Violet Jones
Elias J. Halliday
Rosa E. Benjamin
Corinne R. Azamore

Tomb 10: (THNOC 182) SOCIETY of NATIVES; Debose (Gloria and Herbert)

Societe des Enfants
Etat de la Louisiane. Fondee le 2 Juillet 1870

In Memory of **Herbert A. DeBose**
Born October 30, 1923; died August 29, 1929
God gave, he took, he will restore, he doeth all things well

Gloria J. DeBose
Born August 2, 1930; died September 6, 19(32)

Tomb 11: (THNOC 183) BONSEIGNEAU

Ici reposent
Octave Bonseigneur
Ne le 5 Sept 1832
Decede le 7 Fev, 1856

Marie Rose Escot
Ne (__), decedee le 6 Sept 1866

(__)**Athalie Bonseigneur**
Decedee le 23 Oct 1864

Marianne Bonseigneur
Nee Fournier
Decedee 11 Juin 1871

J. B. D. Bonseigneur
Decedee le 18 Juillet 1871

Emelie Henriette Bonseigneur
Nee Counsin
Decedee le 16 Octobre 1909

Tomb 12: (THNOC 184) LAVIGNE (Alice, Dorothy M., Louise); Brazile (Emily, Frank Sr.); Clayton (Robert Sr.); Leon (Louise); Mello (Lucie M.)

Louis Lavigne
1892 – 1950

Alice Lavigne
1871 – 1955

Emley Brazile
1888 – 1961

Frank Brazile, Sr.
1873 – 1963

Robert H. Clayton, Sr.
1907 – 1967

Dorothy M. Lavigne
1931 - 1983

Tomb 13: (THNOC 185) SOCIETY of ST. IGNACE

Les Enfants de St. Ignace

Tomb 14: (THNOC 186) GRANDPRE (Gardette, Clovis A.)

Clovis A. Grandpre
Died August 1, 1935, aged 75 yrs

Tomb 15: (THNOC 187) CAITONE (alternate spelling Calcone)

Noly P. Caitone
Louisiana
CPL CO F 806 Pioneer Inf
World War I
May 18, 1894 – December 20, 1953

Caitone Family

Tomb 16: (THNOC 188) LUBIN

Tomb 17: (THNOC 189) FORSTALL; Bouise (Anaise Mary Forstall, Emile George, Joseph Eugene, William George); Dave (Joseph Bernard Jr., Joseph Bernard Sr., Mary Ann Bouise, Mary Eloise Goutier); Francis; Lawrence (Arthur Joseph, Elsa Ker, Louise Theonie Forstall; Marquez (Marguerite Lawrence)

J.no F. Therence
Died June 24, 1900, aged 78 yrs

Joseph Eugene Bouise 1915 – 1920
Anaise Mary Forstall Bouise 1874 – 1926

Mary Eloise Goutier Dave 1876 – 1950

William George Bouise 1878 – 1953

Arthur Joseph Lawrence 1884 – 1953

Louise Theonie Forstall Lawrence 1878 – 1957

Elsa Ker Lawrence 1915 – 1969

Joseph Bernard Dave, Jr. 1941 – 1973

Joseph Bernard Dave, Sr. 1912 – 1974

Marguerite Lawrence Marquez 1915 – 1981

Emile George Bouise 1903 – 1989

Mary Ann Bouise Dave 1912 - 2005

Tomb 18: (THNOC 190) SOUBLET (alternate spellings Soublit, Soubie); Barthe (Clemente J.); Brooks (alternate spelling Brooke) (Keisha M.); Marquez (Philomene S.); Saulny (George); Simon (Edward Anthony)

Edwin Anthony Simon
Louisiana
CPL 317 Trench Mortar Btry
World War I
October 22, 1895 – May 10, 1966

George Saulny
Born December 12, 1894; died Nov 17, 1927

Louise Laura Parker
March 18, 1914 - June 21, 1960

George Saulny
(same as above)

Philomene S. Marquez
August 3, 1885 – July 3, 1969

Keisha M. Brooks
February 6, 1972 – July 7, 1996

316

Clement Barthe
Sgt US Army
World War II
1917 - 1983

Tomb 19: (THNOC 191) BOGUILLE (alternate spellings Bougille)
(Roscoe, Sr., Marion, Rosco Jr., Rose); Bernard; Pouplin

William Bernard
Died June 23, 1899, aged 55 years

In loving memory of
Roscoe J. Boguille, Sr. 1913 – 1986

Marion J. Boguille 1914 – 1990

Roscoe J. Boguille, Jr. 1939 – 1994

Rose M. Boguille 1937 – 2008

Steven A. Hester 1969 - 2010

Tomb 20: (THNOC 192) SOCIETY DES ENFANTS DE ST. JOSEPH

Societe Des Enfants de St. Joseph
Instituee le 19 Mars 1849, Par L.A.S.S.L.P.D.L. Ste. V

Ellen Summerville
Decedee le 24 Juillet 1857

Tomb 21: (THNOC 193) SOCIETY AMOUR ETERNAL

Tomb 22: (THNOC 194) SOCIETY LES DAMES DE LA BRANCHE

Societe Des Dames De La Branche
Fondee 10 Sept 1849

Tomb 23: (THNOC 195) SOCIETY OF LOUISIANA; Ciretienne; Society
de la Pouissiniere

Ici Reposent
Lais Bertonneau
Decede le 29 Mars 1840
A l'age de 53 ans

Et su petite fille

Lais Crowell
Decedee le 6 Juillet 1835
A l'age de 6 ans

Dr. J. Chaumette
Decede le 6 Fevrier 1878
A l'age de 58 ans

Tomb 24: (THNOC 196) HALLER (Adolph A., Estelle Marie L.); Foy (Walter J.); Garcia

Walter J. Foy
Died February 18, 1956

Adolph A. Haller
Tec 5 US Army
World War II
1911 - 1976

Tomb 25: (THNOC 197) CASTILLE

Tomb 26: (THNOC 198) ESNARD

Note: The detached tablet was still there in 2015, but illegible.

Tomb 27: (THNOC 199) SOCIETY MOREL; Society of Vin Ferr

Morel

Tomb 28: (THNOC 200) SOCIETY DE JESUS MARIE JOSEPH

Tomb 29: (THNOC 201) BAZANC; PERRAULT

Ici Repose
Ellalie R. J(?)
Nee a la N. Orleans le 20 Ma(?)
Decedee le 11 Mai 1833

Tomb 30: (THNOC 202) HAYDEL (Roy C.); Society of St. John Baptiste

S. J. Baptiste

In memory of my husband
Earl Baines, Sr.
March 19, 1904 – August 28, 1950

( ) and Joseph Ray
Decede le 19 Mai 1893

A l'age de 2 mois

( ) E Circe Boisdore
( ) Esteves ( )
Le 30 Avril 1895

Kenneth C Moore
Louisiana
CPL COH 27 MAR 1 MAR DIV
Vietnam P H
July 3 1947 – March 8, 1968

In memory of
Roy C. Haydel
August 5, 1910 – November 11, 1977

Note: The "Boisdore" above is likely Marie Circe Boisdore, sister of
Arthur Esteves, buried in St. James's Aisle, Tomb 6: (THNOC 33).

Tomb 31: (THNOC 203) LAVIGNE; Gardera (alternate spelling Gardere);
Powhaton

Powhattan James
Born February 10, 1856
Died November 21, 1857

( ) sa Jones
(Two more, in parentheses – no names in THNOC survey)

Marie Louise Mckee
Died Jan 24 1934

Joseph Vallere
Decede le 24 Mai 1818
A l'age de 13 ans

Marie Therese Gardera
Decedee le (5) Avril 1855
A l'age de 99 ans et demie
33 EM

Sully Roudey
Decede le 18 Fevrier 1899
Age de 75 ans

Alfred T. Lavigne, Jr.
March 9, 1925 – October 23, 1994
Alfred T. Lavigne, Sr.
December 20, 1899 – September 11, 1985

Edna J. Lavigne
November 7, 1902 – October 14, 1988

Myrtle M. Clayton
January 7, 1921 – December 1, 1990

Broken tablet:
Nathan (Lavi)gne
October 21, 19( ) - 1986

Florville

Tomb 32: (THNOC 204) LEE; Clayton (Myrtle M.); Ferbos; Gardera
(Maria); Lavigne (Alfred T. Sr., Edna J., Nathaniel L.); Ortus; Roudey
(Sully); Valiere (V. Joseph)

No inscriptions on the tomb. The stone in front says:

Bennie Lee McCall, Jr.
September 10, 1961 - August 30, 1967

My mother
Hermina La Beaud
Died July 22, 1959

Ules La Beaud, Sr.
1915 - 1969

Tomb 33: (THNOC 205) SACRED THOMAS; Dix Freres Sacres;
LaBeaud (Ules Sr.); Mcall (sic) (Bennie Lea Jr.); Thomas

Societe Des Dix Freres Sacres
Fonde en 1845

In loving memory of the **Thomas Family**

Geo. Andre
Died 1928

Amelia Andre
Died 1944

Elmira Thomas
April 6, 1887 – November 14, 1971

August L. Thomas
April 5, 1903 – December 20, 1999

Note: The NAACP pamphlet says that the Societe des Dix Freres Sacres (Ten Sacred Brothers) was founded in 1845, making it "probably the oldest society tomb in Square 3."

Discrepancies
Row M: St. Patrick's Aisle

Tomb 29: The SOC map calls this "28A," making the rest of the numbers from that point on one off of the SOC numbering.

St. John's Aisle, Left (Bienville Alley, Section AL)

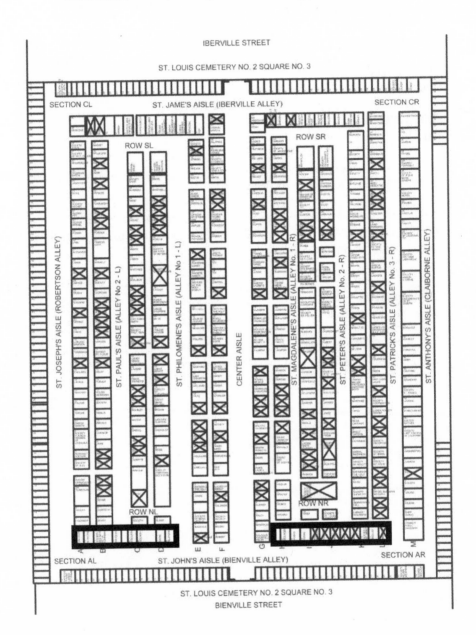

St. John's Aisle (Bienville Alley)

THNOC numbers 165 – 171, 376 - 383

We are numbering from the point of view that we are walking away from the freeway and toward Robertson, with the Bienville entrance on our left and Iberville on our right.

Right Side (Section AR)

Tomb 1: (THNOC 165) Missing tomb, Bellcharo

The tomb was still standing at time of THNOC survey. "Rubble, no tablet."

Tomb 2: (THNOC 166) MOLLAY (alternate spelling Molley, Molly); Populus (Annette Rosemarie)

Famille P. Mollay

Marie Angelina Mollay
Decedeele 28 Fevrier 1849, a l'age de 20 jours (days)

Adelaide Mollay
Decedee le 10 Octobre 1849, a l'age de 23 mois (months)

Auguste Mollay
Decedee le 8 Mai 1854, a l'age de 23 mois (months)

Antoinette Auguste Populus
Decedee le 27 Septembre 1855, a l'age de 43 ans

M. Agnes Mollay
Decedee le 10 Juin 1857, a l'age de 4 mois (months)

Anette Rosemire Populus
Ici Repose

Artemise Lestin
Epouse de Maurice Populus
Nee a le Nlle Orleans cie 1788
Decedee le 9 Novembre 1832

Et
Maurice Populus
Decedee le 15 Juin 1810, age de 72 ans

A. Nelder (stone-cutter)

Tomb 3: (THNOC 167) SOCIETY of ST. BENEDICT

Alfred Joseph

Wilfred M Joseph
Louisiana Pvt Stu Army TNG Corps, World War I
December 10, 1896 – November 22, 1956

Harold G. Heim Sr.
1908 – 1971

Leaning against side:
Elizabeth Duverger
Decedee le 27 Avril 1861
A l'age de 72 ans

Ci-git
Paul Boree
Natif de cette ville
(Native of this city)
Decede le 7 Juillet 1844
A l'age de 70 ans

Tomb 4: Missing tomb, Massnego

(Photo includes missing Tombs 4 – 8)

Tomb 5: Missing tomb, Daal

Tomb 6: Missing tomb, Duplessis

Tomb 7: Missing tomb, Castenede

Tomb 8: Missing tomb, Gaston; March

Tomb 9: (THNOC 168) GOINS; Despinasse

In memory of our mother

Lucia Thomatis Goins
Born September 13, 1884; died July 29, 1971
In memory of our son
August A. Goins
Born January 23, 1908; died May 21, 1939

Father
August J. Goins
Born December 13, 1881; died December 31, 1957

Young Men's Morality B.M.A.A.
Organized July 4, 1897
Incorporated October 19, 1899

Tomb Committee
Henry Baptiste
Jas ( ) Johnson
(ex?) officio
( ) Marcelin
George Robertson
( ) Dejean
Eugene Rouny
Jos. J. Burns
Ernest Burns
V.I. Hardy
Jules Foy
( ) J. Marc( )

Officers
James A. Johnson
Jules Foy
( ) Secretary
Henry Baptiste
( ) Secretary
( ) Maulet
Assistant Secretary
George Robertson
Treasurer

Tomb 10: (THNOC 169) POREE (Alternate spelling Porss; that's how it shows on SOC map)

Tomb 11: (THNOC 170) BOURGEÓIS

R. Bourgeois

A. Labeaud
Died October 17, 1918, aged 26 years

H. Saulmy
Died August 14, 1918, aged 15 years

Geo. Saulmy
Died March 24, 1922, aged 52 years

Norma Maury Saulmy
Born August 17, 1895; died May 20, 1966

Tomb 12: (THNOC 171) CENSUEGOS (alternate spellings Cenfuegos, Cienfuegos, Cienevego)

Luke Ferrand Sr
Louisiana
TEC 5 US Army
World War II
August 17, 1927 – July 1, 1963

Elodie Esquiand
Died May 24 1915, aged 74 yrs

Lloyd and Myrtle Johnston
Ages 18 – 12; died Dec 21 1929

Note: I am assuming they were siblings, who died the same day.

Randolph Jos. Collins
Born November 22, 1927; died June 29, 1944

Alice Esquiano
Died October 11, 1951, aged 71 Yrs

Delandno

John B (De) Rey
Died ( ) 28, 1942

Ici Repose
J. Rollinard Cienevego

Marguerite J. Vigee
July 28, 1906 – August 25, 1977

Rest in Peace
Cenfuegos

Reuben E. McClenon, Jr.
Born May 7, 1934 – Died October 11, 2011

Left Side (Section AL)

Tomb 13: (THNOC 383) BLANCHARD

B. F. Blanchard
1870 – 1921

G. A. Dufauchard
Born September 16, 1907; died March 11, 1928

Chas. Davis
Born December 9, 1877; died December 22, 1928, aged 52 years

Louise Blanchard

Born February 21, 1875; died October 28, 1932

Henry Marcelin
Died September 4, 1933 Age 33

Louis P. Blanchard
1859 – 1935

Felix Lewis
June 8, 1920 – June 14, 1959

Pauline F. Davis
1896 – 1968

Tomb 14: (THNOC 382) BADIE

John Alcindor
Died November 3, 1929 age 29 years

Ci Git
M. Joseph Badie
Decedee le 26 Mai 1832
Agee de 5 ans

Peter Badie, Sr
August 5, 1897 – March 29, 1957

His Beloved Wife

Murtle M. Badie
September 25, 1899 – July 20, 1996

Tomb 15: (THNOC 381) SOCIETY of De Bien Faisance

Olivia Labat
September 7, 1876 – May 2, 1964

In memory of my dear husband
Roland Anthony Orticke
July 11, 1926 – May 1, 1979

In memory of our mother
Hilda Moret Hunter
1913 – 1975

In memory of our mother
Thelma Moret James
1907 - 1972

Juila Moret Wiltz
Novmber 25, 1900 – May 24, 1960

In memory of a dear wife and mother
Eva Labat Vigne
Born August 2, 1898; died December 3, 1957

In memory of a dear husband and father

Arthur Joseph Vigne
Born September 19, 1890; died Dec 6, 1972

Vases inscribed: Mother, Daddy; **James**
Yvonne V. Orticke
1923 - 1998

Grace Moret Bennette
November 14, 1915 – December 2, 1976

Leona Moret Anderson
September 16, 1909 – April 25, 1983

Tomb 16: (THNOC 380) EDOUARDY; Menard

Mme Baptiste Edouary
Nee Marie Louise Menard, native de S. Marc, Ile d'Haiti
Decedee le 13 Fev. 1853 a l'age de 57 ans.

Florville (stone-cutter)

Tomb 17: (THNOC 379) BROULARD (alternate spelling Brulard)

Famille E. Brulard

Marie Beaudequin
Decedee le 12 Juillet 1832
A l'age de 42 ans.

Edouard Brulard
Decedee en 1846 a l'age de 10 Mois.

Henriette Grenier
Epouse d'E. Brulard
Decedee le 8 Juin 1853
A l'age de 32 ans.

Mme Mathilde Antoine
Perraud, nee a Paris France
Decedee le Juillet 1876
A l'age de 60 ans.

Tomb 18: (THNOC 378) SOCIETY DES NATIVES DE LA LOUISIANA

Martin
Decedee le 2 Juin 1861

Societe de Natis
Incorporee le 25 Avril 1872
Nomes des Fondateres Barmarine

Lloyd J. Zimmerman
US Army
Korea
July 28, 1929 – August 18, 2002

In Loving Memory of
Norma Thornton Martin
Born February 18, 1930 – Died September 4, 1949

Anna Coustaut
Born May 26, 1888 – Died August 4, 1964

Lester Martin, Jr.
October 21, 1930 – July 4, 1968

In Loving Memory of
Thelma M. Lyman
"Mama Te"
April 26, 1904 – November 8, 1985

Lionel C. Flot, Sr.
"Buddy"
1899 - 1991

Milford J. Martin
Pvt US Army
World War II
1912 - 1982

In Loving Memory of our Son
Carl Jude Lee
May 6, 1945 – April 19, 1974

Carl Lee
March 12, 1913 – May 15, 1980

Mildred "Sue" Lewis
1912 - 1983

Andrew Lenis, Jr.
US Army
Korea
May 17, 1932 – July 20, 2001

Tomb 19: (THNOC 377) BLANCHARD; Hortense; Duclas

The top section clearly once read "Family" or "Family." The letters are worn, but could spell **"Blanchard."**

Claire Hortense
Nee a St. Marc, Ile St. Domingue
Mort le 30 Aout 1821

A l'age de 54 ans

Victoire Raisin Duclas
Nee a St. Marc, Ile St. Domingue
Mort le 11 Janvier 1811
A l'age de 87 ans

Milton L. Blanchard
Louisiana
Pvt Co C 381 Port BN TC
World War II
September 15, 1898 – July 7, 1965

Note: According to the NAACP pamphlet, the tomb of Claire Hortense and Victoire Duclas is one of the oldest in the cemetery.

Tomb 20: (THNOC 376) VALCOUR (alternate spelling Valcourt, Valcouet); Azemard (alternate spelling Azenard)

Famille Valcour Azenard

Lizzie Miles La Bostrie
Died May 8 1954

Alvin R. La Bostrie
Sgt US Army
World War II
1906 – 1978

Discrepancies
St. John's Aisle

Tomb 1 (THNOC 165) was crossed off on SOC map.

Tomb 12: The SOC map skips Tomb 12. The SOC spreadsheet lists Tomb 12 as Kaery, which appears to be Tomb 2 in Row C)

St. James's Aisle (Iberville Alley, Section CL)

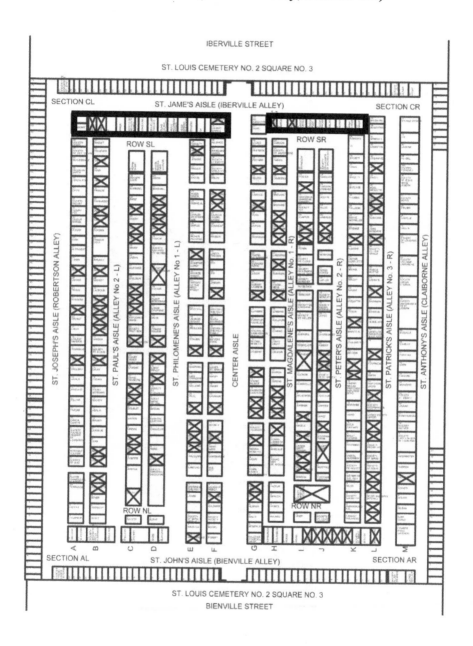

345

St. James's Aisle (Iberville Alley)

THNOC numbers 31 – 38, 238 – 246

We are numbering from the point of view that we are walking away from the freeway and toward Robertson, with the Bienville entrance on our left and Iberville on our right.

Right Side (Section CR)

Tomb 1: (THNOC 38) BAQLET; Saulet

Tomb 2: (THNOC 37) REMY (John); CANONG; Duval

John Remy

1870 – 1927

Emily Canonge
1881 – 1946

Tomb 3: (THNOC 36) BORCEAU; Cornu

Joseph Ferdinand Borgeau
CPL US Army
World War I
July 29, 1895 – January 23, 1976

Tomb 4: (THNOC 35) DELACROIX; Duplessis (Bernadette, Victoria); Roudanez (Rose); Treme (Clement)

Joseph I Delacroix
Louisiana
PFC US Army
World War I
February 1, 1895 – July 21, 1973

Note: According to the NAACP pamphlet, this is also the tomb of Jean Baptiste Roudanez (1815 – 1895), co-founder of the country's first black newspaper, *The New Orleans Tribune*, who also "helped initiate a national campaign for the right of black people to vote."

Tomb 5: (THNOC 34) SOCIETY PROGRES (alternate spelling Le Dames Du Progres)

Le Dames Du Progres

Tomb 6: (THNOC 33) ESTEVES; FLOT (alternate spelling Flote)

Famille
Arthur Esteves

Victor Esteves
December 8, 1874 – July 16, 1961

Laura E. Rillieux
January30, 1884 – August 24, 1964

Louise M. Rillieux
Born March 23, 1908; died January 10, 1960

Lillian M. Ancar
June 26, 1900- June 14, 1967

Camille Brazille Rillieux
Died 12-12-71
Ici Repose

Magdalene Boree
Nee a la Nouvelle Orleans
Decedee le 2 Juillet 1855
A l'age de 60 ans

M. Hortensia Estens
Nee le 9 Mai 1828
Decede le 14 Septembre 1832

Note: According to the NAACP pamphlet, businessman Arthur Esteves, in addition to being a supporter of the Couvent school, was active in the anti-segregation movement. He was involved in bringing the Plessy vs. Ferguson case to the Supreme Court, and published an activist newspaper, *The Crusader*. Born in Haiti, he was born in 1827, and died in 1908.

Tomb 7: (THNOC 32) SOCIETY VIDALIA (alternate spelling Society Vidauary)

Young Men Vidalia B.M.A.A.
Organized

Ici Repose
Laourianno Monroy
Decedee le 22 Janvier 1842
Age de 41 ans
Erige par son beau frère
(Erected by her half-brother)

Mary E. Federow
Wife of Eugene Martin
Born October 13, 1850
Died November 12, 1899
Nicolas Martin
Decedee le 9 Mai 1850
A'lage de 46 ans

Et son epouse
Rose Martin
Native de France
Decedee le 5 Novembre 1881
A l'age de 80 ans

Eugene Martin
April 14, 1841 – July 6, 1908

Tomb 8: Missing tomb, Dridene, Icard (alternate spelling Icaro)

Tomb 9: (THNOC 31) BARDENAV; Herrera; Young Men Vidalia

Young Men Vidalia

Tomb 10: Missing tomb, Bardoville; Caminiere; Chanterelle

Left Side (Section CL)

Tomb 11: (THNOC 238) FOY

Foy

Tomb 12: (THNOC 239) BIENVENIL; no names on spreadsheet

Bienvenu

Ci-Git
J. E. Anne Chena
Mort le 2 Nov 1822
Age de 12 mois

(Marc) Ophlia
Decedee le 12 Nov 1859
A la agee 20 ans

Tomb 13: (THNOC 240) LADIES MORNING STAR SOCIETY (Society of L'Etoile Martin, A298)

Ladies Morning S( ) Society
A. Rodriguez
V. Richard
M. Miles
O. Fortune, Builder
Tomb Committee
Rita Sylvan

Tomb 14: (THNOC 241) LADIES PROGRESSIVE FRIENDS; Society of Naba

Ladies Progressive Friends B.M.A.A.
Organized September 10, 1899
Incorporated February 15, 1900

Building Committee
A. Johnson, Chairlady
M. Trepagnler
E. Rogers
J. Burns
C. Barriere
M. Hobley
C. Hill
C. Isaac
E. Monette
A. J. Ossey, Builder
Officers
E. Barnes, President
W. Johnson, Director
C. Isaac, Vice President
R. J. Pierre, Secretary
S. Johnson, Treasurer

Tomb 15: (THNOC 242) YOUNG FRIENDS OF CHARITY (alternate spelling Society of Chariti)

Young Friends of Charity B.M.A.A.
Organized July 2, 1884
Incorporated September 12, 1884

Officers
C. Richard, Pres
F. Griffin, 1.st V. Pres
J. Blaise, 2.nd
J. Holmes, Jr. Rec Sec
C. D. Henderson Fin
L. L. Peterson Treas
C. J. Southall Coll.

Tomb Committee
A. M. Boutin, Chair
D. J. Rock
J. Henderson
J. A. Delpeach
D. W. Rhodes
J. A. Wilson
C. Weber
V. J. Johnson
A. R. Richard, Sec.

Ci Git
John T. Thomas
Mort le 15 Decembre 1833
Age de (?) ans

Tomb 16: (THNOC 243) DROUELLARD (alternate spelling Drouillar);
LEVELLIER (alternate spelling Leveille)

Tomb 17: (THNOC 244) BONSEIGNEUR

Note: This plaque is on the ground in between Tombs 17 and 18; nor listed on any map.

Marguerite Vigne McConnell
May 4, 1910 – December 12, 2002

Tomb 18: (THNOC 245) SOCIETE DES ENFANTS DU SILENCE

Societe Des Enfants Du Silence B A A M
Organized le 1.R. F.R 1892 (first of February?)
Incorporated le 12 S.R 1892 (Septembre)

Tomb 19: (THNOC 246) ERNEST; Armand; Cloud

Joseph Ernest
Beloved husband of Antonia Baquet Ernest
May 3, 1878 – July 4, 1941

Ici repose
Charles (?) Indon
(?)re Henderson

Tomb 20: Missing tomb. No name on SOC map, but not crossed off. No THNOC number.

(Photo includes missing Tombs 20 – 22)

Tomb 21: Missing tomb, Romain (alternate spelling Roman)

Tomb 22: Missing tomb, Majere

Wall Vaults, Section A (St. John's Aisle, Bienville Alley)

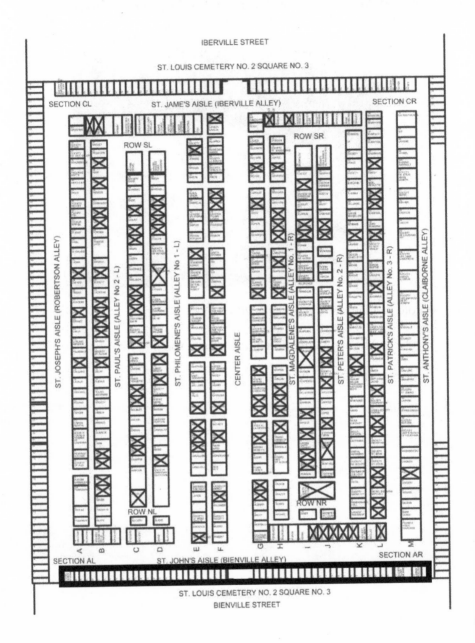

Wall Vaults, St. Anthony's Aisle, Section A

Walking away from Claiborne and toward Robertson, with the entrance/Bienville to the left, on the other side of the wall, and Iberville to the right. St. John's Aisle (Bienville Alley) runs along the left.

When you enter the cemetery from Bienville, the wall vaults on the right-side are designated on the SOC map as Section AR; the wall vaults on the left-hand side are designated on the SOC map as Section AL.

50 vaults total

There are no names or dates listed in the SOC spreadsheets for any of the wall vaults on Wall A, with the following exceptions.

Section AR

Tomb 1: **(THNOC 173)** LADIES SECURITY; Society of Damos Demois

Ladies Security B. A.

Tomb 2: **(THNOC 172)** SOCIETY of FLEUR DE MARIE

Societe Fleur de Marie Sous La
De Stanne Instituee le 15 D

Wall Tombs

Section AL

Tomb 50: **(THNOC 375)** LADIES & YOUNG LADIES VETERANS

Corner of Bienville and Robertson

Ladies and Young Ladies Veterans B.M.A.A.

Organized July 6, 1893
Incorporated Aug 4, 1896
No inscriptions on any vaults. In lower left hand corner the following
inscription:

Building Committee
E. Holmes Chairlady
L. Rowe Ex Officio
L. M. Hobbs
I. Bell
A. Guichard
M. Maurice
M. H. Edmonds
J. Richard
C. Luchi
Jos. N. Cheri
J. Capas Builder

Wall Tombs

Wall Vaults, Section B (St Anthony's Aisle, Claiborne Alley)

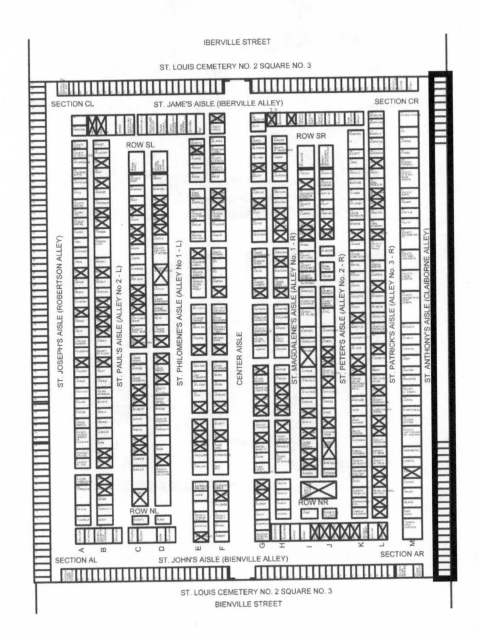

Wall Vaults, St. Anthony's Aisle, Section B

Walking away from Bienville and toward Iberville, with Robertson to the left and Claiborne to the right. St. Anthony's Aisle, Row M, is directly to our left.

76 vaults total

Vault 3: **John Edward Barjon**, died 1/4/1972, age 64; **Armand J. Peron**, died 1/17/1944

Vault 10: **Henry Paul Decou**, died 5/31/19655, age 67; **Paul Sigg**, died 11/11/1941; **Sidney Sigg**, died 12/28/1960, age 73

Vault 11: **Louise Ferrrand**, died 3/1/1943, age 74; **Naomi and Manuel Ferrand**; **Sidney St. Martin**, died 2/4/1967, age 69

The vaults between 21 and 66 are blank on the SOC map; on the THNOC map they're listed as "Condemned."

Wall Vaults, Section C (St. James's Aisle, Iberville Alley)

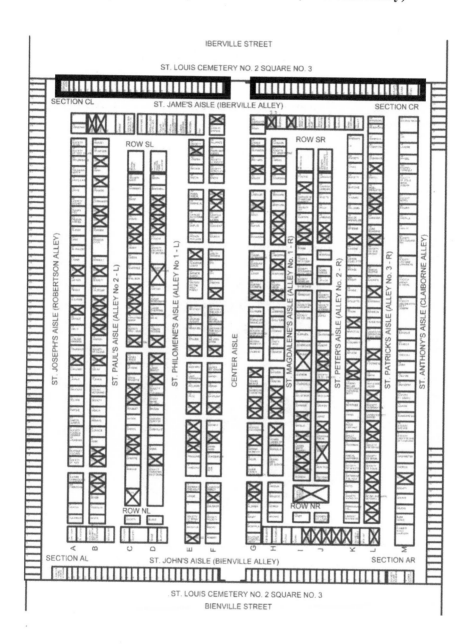

Wall Vaults, St. James's Aisle, Section C

Walking away from Claiborne and toward Robertson, with the entrance/Bienville to the left, and Iberville to the right, on the other side of the wall. St. James's Aisle (Iberville Alley) is directly to our left.

The wall vaults on the right-side are designated on the SOC map as Section CR; the wall vaults on the left-hand side of St. Louis Aisle (Center Aisle) are designated on the SOC map as Section CL.

3 tombs at the start of Section CR, and 1 tomb at the end of Section CL.

47 wall vaults:

Righthand Side, Section CR

Tomb 1: (THNOC 207) PERET; Hypolite

Ici Reposent
Euphemie Peret
Decedee le 1. Juillet 1816

Et sa mere
Charlotte Peret
Decedee le 25 Nov 1856

Hellen August
Died April 21, 1929

August Martin
Died July 20 1945

Rosa Vols
Died December 5, 1938

Emma Martin
Died May 17, 1960

Jack August
Died April 2, 1958

Adele Adolphe
Died May 26, 1968

Tomb 2: (THNOC 206) OLIVER

Famille B. Olivier

John Woods, Sr.   **1837 – 1900**

Numa O. Woods, Jr.   **1907 – 1924**

Ernestine C. Woods   **1852 – 1926**

Albert Woods, Sr.   **1874 – 1930**

Sidney M. Saulet   **1903 – 1970**

Numa O. Woods, Sr.   1882 – 1979

Callico

Tomb 3: (THNOC 205A) SOCIETY ST. CECILE

Incorporee le 6 Juin 1868

Righthand Side, Section CR

Vault 15: **Dame Celestine Glapion**, died 1877 (note: née Marie Charles); **Ferdinand Delpit**, died 1930; **Famille Glapion**

Vault 17: **Geo. A. Jollio**, died 1954; **Lucien L. Ancelin**; **Olympe Foster**, died 1940

Vault 18: **Louis Jones**; **Marie Harney**, died 1920

Vault 19: **Camille St. Arge; Nini** (no last name), died age 11; **Marie Micline**, died at age 100

Vault 22: **Angela Nicolas; Charlotte Dolliole**

Lefthand Side, Section CL

Vault 23: **Constance Louise Laurant,** 11/21/1818

Vault 25: **Emile** (no last name); **Pauline** (no last name)

Vault 26: **Antoine Clements; Joseph Bell**

Vault 27: **Rosalie Chesheau,** died 1833

Vault 28: **Emillie Lecoxtt,** died 1863; **Emily Ally; Josephine Zamora,** died 1885; **Magdeline Zamora,** died1833

Vault 29: **Isnard** (This may be the signature of the stone-cutter, or someone named Isnard may be interred here)

Vault 30: **Cora Girodeaux** (note: mere); **Louis Girod; Louisine Girodeaux** (note: epouse); **Mary L. Betholine; Robert Corner, Jr.,** died 1966

Vault 31: **Jules Dessalles,** died 7/13/1810, at age 32; **Marie Victoire Fazende,** died 9/30/1833, at ge 70

Vault 32: **Bernard Castelin,** 1833; **Joseph Pepin, Jr.,** 1915

Vault 33: **F.N. Seligo__r**

Vault 34: **Honorine** 1831 (note: daughter of Honorine)

Vault 35: **Adele G. Marant**, 1965; **Charlotte Paul**, 1857, age 70; **Jacques Ferrand**, 7/24/1852; Family of **Andrew Gasparini**; **Society of St. James**

Vault 37: **Joseph Hardy**, 1927

Vault 39: **Mervin J. Brochard**, 1973; **Famille Louis LeGros**

Vault 40: **Jordan Noble**; **Susane Macarty**, 1840, age 95; **O'Brien Family**

Vault 41: **J.P. Percy**, 1844

Vault 42: **A. Aurelia Dinet**, 1839; **Pierre Blazo**, 1837

Vault 43: **Emile Pierre Carmel**; **Favre**

Vault 44: **Edmond Dolliole**, 1939; **Simon Dolliole**, 12/2/1919

Tomb 4: **(THNOC 339)** SOCIETY DES ENFANTS DE ST. JEAN

Wall Vaults, Section D (St. Joseph's Aisle, Robertson Alley)

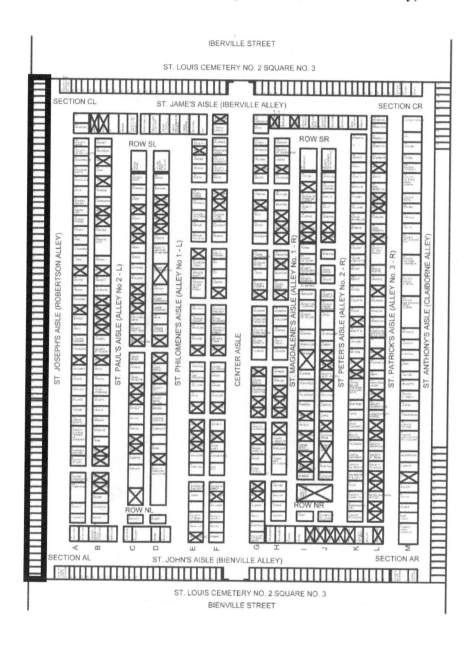

Wall Vaults, St. Joseph's Aisle, Section D

Walking away from Bienville and toward Iberville, with Robertson to the left, just over the wall, and Claiborne to the right. St. Joseph's Aisle, Row A, is directly to the right.

76 vaults total.

Vault 2: **Lucie Camille; Ecaraux**

Vault 3: **Joseph A. Bazile; Larry Bundy; A. C. Glapion; Emma Glapion; Grace D. Vea**

Vault 4: **Alfred** ?

Vault 7: **Eulalie E.L.** Baranier; Lucien Broussard; Francois Muro; Francois Muro, Jr.; Emile Thezan

Vault 8: **Jean Baptiste; Joseph Bazile,** died 11/2/1966, age 84; **Martin Duplessis,** died 1948, age 71; **Hortense Hubbard; Theres Hubbard,** died 1928, age 10 mos; **William Hubbard; Mrs. Joseph Magloire; Peter Reine**

Vault 10: **Eloise Edmond Hewlett**

Vault 11: **Famille J.A.** Welder; **Henry Ferrand; Antoinette Prevost; Louis Tougard**

Vault 12: **Clarence Amedee Clarence; Walter Figaro; Marie Lawrence; Lester L. Picou, Sr.**

Vault 13: **Louise Etienne; Eugene Fraisinette; John Ripoll; John Ripoll; Joseph Ripoll; Joseph Ripoll; Manuel Ripoll**

Vault 14: **Dame Francinette; Ferdinand Laserre**

Vault 15: **Edward Pinkney; James H.Pinkney**

Vault 16: **Andre Gregoire; Toulme**

Vault 17: **Antoine Blandin**

Vault 18: **Sabin** ?; **Sylvere Capo; Leocaine Flavie; Stanley Saulny, Jr.**

Vault 19: **Auguste or Augustin (sic) Love; Felicite Montreuil; A. Celanie Rebuffet**

Vault 20: **Hilda Fabre Abatte,** died 4/10/1971; **E. Fabre,** died 3/11/1926; **F. Fabre,** died 5/31/1942; **J. Fabre,** died 7/15/1954; **M. Fabre,** died 1/3/1954; **Marcelle Fabre,** died 5/6/1969

Vault 22: **Fernandez**

Vault 23: **Zoe Marie Payet Reimoneng**

Vault 24: **Rose Fortin; Gutierrez; Elaine Reimoneng,** died 9/28/1842

Vault 26: **Pauline Gaiennie; Alice L. Glapion**, died 1963; **Joseph Glapion**, died 1967; **James Guichard**, died 1913; **Innocente T. Larrieu**, died 1899; **Louis D. Larrieu**, died 1921; **Olivia Larrieu**, died 7/9/1938; **Dame Heloise Pre**, died 1856
Note: The names for this tomb are followed by the note: "27?" This is a possible mixup in tomb numbers.

Vault 27: **Burns Family**; **Leonie Galle**, died 7/9/1960; **Lucien Galle**, died 4/2/1956
Note: The names for this tomb are followed by the note: "28?" This is a possible mixup in tomb numbers.

Vault 28: **George Burns**, died 10/18/1930; **Escarpontier; Alice Fortuné**, died 4/16/1914; **Lionel Fortuné**, died 10/8/1965; **William Nimtz**, died 12/25/1968
Note: The names for this tomb are followed by the note: "29?" This is a possible mixup in tomb numbers.

Vault 29: **Marie Doyle Bernal**, died 1967; **Raoul J. Bernal**, died 1950;Note: The names for this tomb are followed by the note: "30?" This is a possible mixup in tomb numbers.

Vault 30:**John**, died 11/1/1935; **Ama** "Fille"; **Antoinette Robert**

Vault 31: **Stella Adams**; **L. Lavoux**, died 10/6/1918
Note: This may be a transcription error, and the same L. Lavoux listed in Vault 33. Ancestry.com shows one Lucien Lavoux (or LaVoux) who died 10/16/1918.

Vault 32: **Marie Bose Baptiste; Juliet Meteye**, died 6/26/1915

Vault 33: **L. Lavoux**, died 10/6/1918
Note: This maybe the the same L. Lavoux listed in Vault 33. See note above.

Vaut 34: **Guy Duplantier; William Duplantier; D. Joseph; Valsin Larche; Larche Valsin; Emma Willoz**, died 10/1/1857; **Emma Willoz**, died 1837, age 35
Note: "Valsin Larche" and "Larche Valsin" are listed that way in the THNOC survey. "Valsin Larche" was the correct name, going by Ancestry.com. The other may be a notation for his widow.

Vault 35: **Famille Peche; Pierre Peche**, died 1/9/1914; **Felicite**, "Vve."

Vault 36: **Marie Helene**; died 3/23/1858

Vault 38: **Marie Fse Riveron**, died 7/22/1858

Vault 39: **Rosette Montreuil**

Vault 40: **Desiree; Rosalie**

Vault 41: **Mrs. O. Balthazar**, died 8/6/1934; **Henry P. Figare**, died 7/25/1987; **Mrs. John Lalunier**, died 4/28/198?.; **Josephine**, died 5/26/1863

Vault 42: **W.D. Anthony Augusti Born; Emily Caruthers; Douxbarierre**, died 7/12/1851; **Edouard Dountraneret Gaignard**, died 2/7/1814; **Annie Robinson**, 58 years; **Emily Robinson**, died 10/6/1918; **George Robinson**, died 4/8/1859; **Robinson** (no first name)

Vault 43: **Lussan Alabau; Marie**, died 8/12/1873

Vault 44: **Aussan; S. Joseph**

Vault 46: **Uranie Branard**, died 4/3/1859; **Ules Coste**, died 10/9/1964; **Claire Jerome; Elizabeth Latrini**, died 4/23/1862; **Mary L. Lyons**, died 5/7/1900; **Suzanne Mercier**, died 12/16/1814; **Francis J. Moss**, died 6/1878; **Mari L. Moss**, died 10/23/1890; **Theodele Reusse**

Vault 47: **Louis Angelo Ferrand**, died 8/8/1879

Vault 48: **Caroline Proctor**, died 1815; **A. (Proctor?)**, died 8/18/1859, "ma fille"

Vault 49: **Amelie Barq; Marionni Baurie; Adolphe Daunes; Leonise H. Duncey**

Vault 50: **Elisa Boulete**, died 2/25/1869; born in the Parish of St. Landry (age 8 yrs); **Dora Gavillin** (?), died 1971; **La Famile A. Bon**, a ma Mere; **Montegut Family; Louis P. Usmin**, died 6/13/1840; **Pierre Usmin**, died 3/14/1845; **????** (sic), died 10/29/1859, "mere"

Vault 52: **Ferrand; Emelile** (?) (sic) Landry, died 1/11/1860, age 28 years; **Daniel**

Vault 54: **Marie Antoinette**, died 9/25/1871, 53 ans; **Philippe Joseph**, died 8/1853, 8 yrs old; **Rose Marceline Rose**, died 2/1861 (Signature: Daniel Warburg)

Vault 55: **Joseph DeLille**, died 9/29/1845

Vault 57: **Alice Duhamel**, died 4/2/1866; **Pedro Sierra**, died 5/14/1877

Vault 58: **Family Glapion; Mirsine Fih** (?) (sic), died 1846; **Martin-Hamis**

Vault 59: **Bennie Glapion**

Vault 61: **Famille Balthazar; Famille Joachim Lewis; Hamilton C. Lewis; Joachim Lewis**

Vault 62: **Mary Bennett; Dorothea Brewster**, died 3/10/1961; **Marie Johns; Jean Marie**

Vault 63: **Marie Daniel**

Vault 64: **William Epps, Sr.; Armand Vincent**

Vault 65: **Loussune Casti-Tart; Marie Doulet; Denise Duplessis; Eugene Duplessis; J. Leconte; Susan Landell; Alice Tio**, died 8/21/1957

Vault 66: **Marie Elizabeth; John Haller**

Vault 67: **Mathieu Famille; Annele Wietz; Joswitz; Josephine Wietz**

Vault 68: **Antoinette Boussou; Louise Emillien**

Vault 69: **Joseph Leon Duminy; M. Joseph Leon Duminy**

Vault 70: **Hortansia Bouyer; Mathilie L. Desdunes**

Vault 71: **Charles Mony**

Vault 72: **Antonia Alice Duplantier; Marie Philomene Rigeaux**

Vault 73: **Justine Alexander; Mme J. B.Alexis; Theresa Avegno** (alternate name Avengo)

Vault 74: **Jeanne Aline; Frank Avegno; Rosine Comtesse; Eva Longpré; Macarty; Paul**

Vault 75: **Mary Bernard; Mary Beatrix Cagette; Mary Duplantier; Seraphine Rabrance Foster; Albert Haydel; Andrew Jefferson; Mrs. E. C. Simmons; Simmons**

Vault 76: **Matilda Beauregard; Carlo Hart,** died 10/30/1933; **Litty; Lanusse; Litty; Edward Reed; Edward**

Listed in Row D, but no Vault number given:

Irma Lars Semansian, died 4/8/1858

Stone Cutters

Callico (J.F. Callico)
Row I, Tomb 17 (THNOC 73)
Row L, Tomb 15 (THNOC 155)
Row L, Tomb 38 (THNOC 139)
Wall Vault Section C, Tomb 2 (THNOC 206)

F. J. Duplessis Fondateur
Row K, Tomb 29 (THNOC 130)

Florville (Florville Foy)
Row B, Tomb 2 (THNOC 317)
Row B, Tomb 4 (THNOC 319). Tomb is missing; tablet is propped at
Tomb 3 (THNOC 318).
Row B, Tomb 32 (THNOC 335)
Row F, Tomb 19 (THNOC 222)
Row F, Tomb 20 (THNOC 223)
Row G, Tomb 1 (THNOC 1)
Row H, Tomb 5 (THNOC 58)
Row I, Tomb 23 (THNOC 79)
Row J, Tomb 10 (THNOC 99). At the time of the 1983 Tablet Survey,
there were tablets signed both "Florville" and "Monsseaux and Trinchard"
noted on this tomb.Row K, Tomb 26 (THNOC 128)
Row M, Tomb 31 (THNOC 203)
St. John's Aisle, Tomb 16 (THNOC 380)

Isnard (John Jacques Isnard)
Row F, Tomb 29 (THNOC 231)
Row H, Tomb 19 (THNOC 48). Tomb is missing.
Row J, Tomb 25 (THNOC 90)
Wall Vaults Section C, Vault 29. It's unclear if this is the work of Isnard,
or the name of the person buried here.

J. Karcher (Karcher Marble Works)
Row M, Tomb 2: (THNOC 175)

Monsseaux (written as Mousseau and Monsseaus))Paul Hippolyte
Monsseaux)
Row A, Tomb 10 (THNOC 365) (transcribed as Mousseau)
Row H, Tomb 13 (THNOC 54)
Row I, Tomb 31 (THNOC 84) (transcribed as Monsseaus)
Row J, Tomb 10 (THNOC 99). At the time of the 1983 Tablet Survey,

there were tablets signed both "Florville" and "Monsseaux and Trinchard" noted on this tomb.

Alex Nelder
Row D, Tomb 15 (THNOC 284)
Row K, Tomb 23 (THNOC 125)
St. John's Aisle, Tomb 2 (THNOC 166)

Trinchard
Row J, Tomb 10 (THNOC 99). At the time of the 1983 Tablet Survey, there were tablets signed both "Florville" and "Monsseaux and Trinchard" noted on this tomb.

Daniel Warburg
Wall Vaults Section D, Vault 54.

Afterword: My Life at Square 3

People have been curious about why I took on this particular project. I'm not from New Orleans. I'm not from the South, having lived in Minnesota and North Dakota all my life. I'm not African-American. I'm not even Catholic! So where did all this come from?

The dead have always been friendly to me. I played in the cemetery when I was a little girl; I took refuge there from the upheavals of life as a teenager; and as an adult, I visit and photograph cemeteries everywhere I visit. This comes so naturally and obviously to me that I completely forget anyone might find it morbid, and when they do, I'm always surprised. So I'm not a person who visited New Orleans and fell in love with its cemeteries; I fell in love with the cemeteries, and that's why I visited New Orleans in the first place.

I'd been researching folk magic and folk religion, and read about Marie Laveau's tomb in St. Louis #1, which led to various photography books about New Orleans' above-ground cemeteries. When my future husband first came to my apartment, the first thing he saw was a picture of the Laveau tomb, printed off the Internet, which was right inside the front door. Little did I know what the future would bring!

When I finally set foot in St. Louis #1, the reality was better than I could have dreamed. In fact, my first thought was "I could live here." Later the same day, I went back to St. Louis #1 for a tourist tour, and, having a little extra time to fill, the guide took us down the street, to St. Louis #2, to see another reputed tomb of Marie Laveau. St. Louis #2 was just as beautiful, but even more melancholy. St. Louis #1 had bustled with tourists and film crews, but St. Louis #2, at that moment, was otherwise empty, with an air of neglect. The ravages of "urban renewal" – with the freeway practically on top of it, and, post-Katrina, the nearby housing projects already slated for their eventual demolition – left it feeling lonelier, surrounded by the ghost of the neighborhood that once surrounded it.

Going back a few days later, I looked at the tombs, some of them hardly more than piles of rubble, and I began to wonder who was in them. And thus I began from the opposite side of most researchers, who are looking for the tomb of a particular person.

Back home in Fargo, I started gathering information. The Save Our Cemeteries organization emailed me their maps and spreadsheets of all three Squares, and gave me information on their joint survey with The Historic New Orleans Collection (1981 – 1983), which preserved the inscriptions then visible on the tombs. By the time I got back to New Orleans to start on the project, though, I realized that I had no confidence in my ability to carry it through. I put off going to the cemetery I was there specifically to visit. "I'm not a researcher," I wrote from my French

Quarter hotel. I was a poet who worked at a public library, and those weren't really qualifications for this kind of thing.

The next day, I walked down to the Treme Cultural Center for a Second Line. I saw two young African-American women, maybe in their teens, weaving through the crowd. They wore matching black t-shirts with giant, bright gold letters that read: "No past, no future."

That inspired me to follow up on my plan. I went to the cemetery and started taking photos, marking their positions on the map. Then, sweaty and disheveled, I walked over to THNOC. They got out a big map, which showed the numbers of the tombs that correlated them with the Tablet Survey cards, and then I went to the microfilm reader.

When I saw the detail on the cards, it was obvious that a lot of information they recorded, which was still visible on the tombs in the early '80s, had since been lost to the naked eye. For more tombs than I expected, it would in fact be possible to look at a tomb and find out the names of people buried there, even for many that are now in much worse condition. All it would take would be some cross-referencing.

I said to myself, "I can do that!" If all I could do was to make the information slightly easier to find, for future genealogical and historical researchers, that would still be a worthwhile thing to do. Since that moment, I've never doubted the value of the project.

Despite being drawn to its feeling of neglect, I don't blame anyone for the condition of the cemetery or any of its tombs. It's just time. If St. Louis #2 proves anything, it's that time passes, and what seems solid and secure is fleeting. As a rule, Americans don't like to acknowledge the damage that time can do. In the Upper Midwest, where I'm from, a lot of things get torn down before they have the chance to accrete any history around them. In St. Louis #2, you can see what will happen to everything, if we don't love it enough to hold back entropy.

After all, these tombs weren't cheap. Someone cared very much about the people who went into them. They were real people, with whole lives, and they created this amazing city that we love. Then the people who loved them died, too. Historical forces caused changes in the city, which in turn affected the cemetery.

It's wonderful to see the tombs that show recent use, which shows that the occupants are being taken care of. But I care most about the people no one is looking for. Maybe someone would be looking for them, if more people knew where they were. Maybe the person looking for them hasn't been born yet.

With the tombs that have been renovated, and that are in current use, I have a lot of concern to show no disrespect to the families. But in the back of my mind, I'm always remembering that a hundred-plus years from now, people may be looking for them, too. Great-grandchildren will want to find their great-grandparents, and anything can happen between now and then.

Of course the names here barely begin to list everyone buried in Square 3. When I learned about the existence of old Internment Records, my heart raced, but what I could access were microfilmed scans of ledgers, handwritten in faint pencil –in French. For someone, this might lead to fruitful further research.

At least these names are a start. In the end, everyone who ever lived is important. Maybe I can't do anything much in the larger scale of things, but I can do something for what people I can, in this particular spot on the planet.

I am forever in the debt of the folks at Save Our Cemeteries: in the abstract, since the group originally formed to protect the wall vaults in Square 3, which would otherwise have been torn down, and in particular. Former Executive Director Angie Green sent me the SOC maps and spreadsheets in about five minutes after my initial email, and was a wonderful source for my many follow-up questions. The current Executive Director, Amanda Walker, has also been very helpful and encouraging, and gracefully agreed to write a foreword for this book.

I also need to thank the patient people at The Historic New Orleans Collection. That includes Jessica Dorman, their Director of Publications, who has been very supportive, and especially the staff at the Williams Research Center. I'm pretty sure they could tell I'm not a professional researcher, but they did their best to make me feel at home.

Resources for Further Study, and Bibliography

The Historic New Orleans Collection
www.hnoc.org
Williams Research Center
410 Chartres Street
New Orleans LA 70130
Phone: 504-598-7171
Email: wrc@hnoc.org
Hours: Tuesday - Saturday, 9:30 am - 4:30 pm. Closed holidays.

New Orleans Public Library
www.neworleanspubliclibrary.org
Louisiana Division
219 Loyola Ave
New Orleans LA 70112
Phone: 504-596-2560
Email: archivist@neworleanspubliclibrary.org
Hours: Monday - Thursday, 10:00 am - 8:00 pm; Friday - Saturday, 10:00 am - 5:00 pm; Sunday, 1:00 pm - 5:00 pm. Closed holidays.

Save Our Cemeteries
saveourcemeteries.org
1539 Jackson Avenue
Suite 415
New Orleans LA 70130-5896
Phone: 504-525-3377
Email: soc@saveourcemeteries.org
Hours: Monday – Friday, 9:00 am – 5:00 pm. Closed holidays.

The University of Pennsylvania has done a comprehensive guide to St. Louis #1, called Dead Space, utilizing GIS tools. They have another, Dead Space II, in the works for St. Louis #2, so keep an eye out for that. (See their web page at https://www.design.upenn.edu/historic-preservation/work/dead-space-ii-st-louis-cemetery-no1-new-orleans).

You'll also want to look up the photos on the Find a Grave website (https://new.findagrave.com/). The majority of the St. Louis Cemetery #2 photos were taken by a woman named Donna Dinstel, who's provided an excellent resource.

Bibliography

Arrigo, Jan, and Laura A. McElroy. *Cemeteries of New Orleans: A Journey through the Cities of the Dead*. Stillwater, MN: Voyageur Press, 2005.

Blue Book. Applewood Books, 2013.

Brock, Eric J. *New Orleans Cemeteries*. Charleston, SC: Arcadia, 1999.

Brothers, Thomas D. *Louis Armstrong's New Orleans*. New York: W.W. Norton & Co, 2007.

Cassimere, Raphael, Joseph Logsdon, and Donald C. Hardy. *History of St. Louis Ii Cemetery*. New Orleans: New Orleans NAACP, 1980.

Conrad, Glenn R, and Earl F. Niehaus. *Cross, Crozier, and Crucible: A Volume Celebrating the Bicentennial of a Catholic Diocese in Louisiana*. New Orleans: Published by the Archdiocese of New Orleans in cooperation with the Center for Louisiana Studies, 1993.

"Creole History & Genealogy." CreoleGen.org. Web.

Crutcher, Michael E. *Tremé: Race and Place in a New Orleans Neighborhood*. Athens, Ga: Univ. of Georgia Press, 2010.

Desdunes, Rodolphe L. *Our People and Our History: Fifty Creole Portraits*. Baton Rouge: Louisiana State University Press, 2001.

Florence, Robert, and Mason Florence. *New Orleans Cemeteries: Life in the Cities of the Dead*. New Orleans, La: Batture Press, 1997.

Gehman, Mary, and Lloyd Dennis. *The Free People of Color of New Orleans: An Introduction*. Donaldsonville, LA: Margaret Media, 2003.

Gehman, Mary, and Nancy Ries. *Women and New Orleans: A History*. New Orleans, LA: Margaret Media, 1988.

Kein, Sybil. *Creole: The History and Legacy of Louisiana's Free People of Color*. Baton Rouge: Louisiana State Univ. Press, 2002.

Ochs, Stephen J. *A Black Patriot and a White Priest: André Cailloux and Claude Paschal Maistre in Civil War New Orleans*. Baton Rouge: Louisiana State University Press, 2000.

"Sisters of the Holy Family." www.sistersoftheholyfamily.com. Web.

Survey of Historic New Orleans Cemeteries, MSS 360, Williams research Center, The Historic New Orleans Collection

Thompson, Shirley E. *Exiles at Home: The Struggle to Become American in Creole New Orleans*. Cambridge, Mass: Harvard University Press, 2009.

Wilson, Samuel, Mary L. Christovich, and Roulhac Toledano. *New Orleans Architecture: Volume III: The Cemeteries*. Gretna [La.: Pelican Pub. Co, 1971.

Wilson, Samuel, Mary L. Christovich, and Roulhac Toledano. *New Orleans Architecture: Volume VI: Faubourg Tremé and the Bayou Road*. Gretna [La.: Pelican Pub. Co, 1971.

Wilson, Samuel, and Leonard V. Huber. *The St. Louis Cemeteries of New Orleans*: New Orleans, La: St. Louis Cathedral, 1963.

About the Author

Karen Joan Kohoutek has published *The Jack-o-Lantern Box*, a novella about a small town Halloween, and *Votive: Poems and Oracle*, through the Skull and Book Press. Her essays on weird fiction and pulp writers have appeared in various journals and literary blogs, and been presented at a PCA/ACA (Popular Culture Association/American Culture Association) conference, as well as at the Armitage Symposium at NecronomiCon Providence 2017. Recently, her essay on St. Louis #2 was published in *The AGS Quarterly: Bulletin of the Association for Gravestone Studies*. Her own blog can be found at octoberzine.blogspot.com. She lives in Fargo, ND.

(Photo courtesy of Nicole Hofer).